Do What Works

The B2B Ads Handbook

Your portable B2B ads agency

Kevin Lord Barry

Right Side Up Press
Riverhead, NY

Paperback ISBN: 979-8-9994954-0-2
Ebook ISBN: 979-8-9994954-1-9

Book cover design by Right Side Up Studio
Book interior design by Jess LaGreca, Mayfly book design

Library of Congress Catalog Number: 2025914594

First Printing: 2025

Contents

Foreword ix

How to Use this Book 1

What you'll learn 1

What you'll achieve 1

How Ads Fit Into Marketing Strategy 3

Why ads matter more than ever 3

Potential B2B Ad Outcomes 4

Strategic Takeaways 6

B2B Advertising 101 7

Advertising vs. marketing vs. sales 7

The age of iteration 9

B2B vs. B2C 10

Strategic Takeaways 11

The Levers of B2B Advertising 13

The Four Levers of B2B Advertising 13

Lever 1—Audience: Targeting Your Target Market 17

Google 19

Social 20

The 3 Ad Platform Targeting Strategies 20

The Three Main B2B Audience Segments 24

Targeting Enterprise Audiences (Traditional B2B) 24

ABM 29

Channel for enterprise 32

Sales > marketing 32

Offer for enterprise 34

Creative best practices for enterprise 34

Targeting Small Business Audiences (B2SMB) 35

Targeting Micro-Business Audiences (B2MicroB) 37

Targeting by Vertical 39

Learning From Other Marketing Channels **41**

Lever 2—Offer : Give your audience what they want **43**

It's in the name 43

Offer types 44

Nailing your offer 45

The antidote to ad fatigue 45

How's your Funnel? 47

Troubleshooting your offer 50

Lever 3—Conversion Event: Train Your Team and the Algorithm . . **53**

What is a conversion event? 53

What's the value of a lead? 54

Marketers need to Create L.I.F.E 54

Rules for conversion events 55

Channel considerations 57

What if I'm not getting the leading indicators I want? 57

Pick up the phone for intent 58

How Advertising Differs for Sales-led vs Product-led Companies . . . 58

Lever 4—Creative : Talk to your audience the right way **61**

If advertising were a restaurant 61

We're not hawking toasters 61

Visual headlines for the win 63

Be specific 64

Why 9? 65

Testing copy is like playing Battleship 66

Creative drives lead quality 67

Qualification through your competitors 67

Don't talk about yourself 67

Keep the offer in the headline 68

Clever doesn't work, but unexpected can 68

You are interrupting 68

There's a time and a place for jargon 69

You need a system to review ads 70

There are three big barriers to getting creative tested 70

Check your in-house ego 71

Create LIFE with campaign consolidation 71

What else works? 72

On writing well 74

Recap: The Levers of B2B Advertising 76

Channel-specific guides **77**

Channel myths BUSTED! 78

The Power of LinkedIn Ads **81**

Robust targeting 81

Hands on (in good ways and bad) 81

Maximum Delivery (Don't do it) 82

Why is LinkedIn so expensive? 82

Getting started on LinkedIn 83

Control 84

Beware of "or" statements 84

Don't overdo it 84

Strategic Takeaways 85

The Magic of SEM (Google) **87**

Even Google doesn't know how Google works 87

Google keeps us in business 87

High intent = low-hanging fruit 88

Saturation—or—scrapping the bottom of the funnel 89

Intent alignment 89

3 types of keywords 90

Overview of the three keyword types 91

Quality leads? Search no further 91

Go broad only when you have a conversion signal

(no matter what Google says) 92

What does a good conversion signal look like? 93

Match type and keyword intent 94

Keyword type 94

Google and the "E"-word 95

Impression share 96

Growth opportunities 98

Volume and net new inventory 99

A word about the auction 100

Impression share AKA the 800-pound gorilla 100

Strategic Takeaways 101

Meta-Facebook & Instagram Ads for B2B 103

    Why Facebook targeting is counterintuitive 103

    Conversion signal is everything on Facebook 104

    Let the algorithm ride 104

    Junk leads 104

    Impression share 105

    Broad targeting & First party data 105

    Advantage Plus Audiences 106

    Strategic Takeaways 107

Strategy 109

    Postmortem questions following an underperforming campaign . . 109

B2B Attribution Guidelines 111

    How confident are you in your tracking and attribution? 111

    First click, multi-click, and more 112

    Attribution Best Practices 112

    Making multitouch work 113

    Strategic Takeaways 114

Testing 115

    Apples to apples 115

    Testing outside of ad learning 116

    Testing best practices 116

    How to do brand advertising the right way 118

    Payback Window Affects Strategy 119

    Strategic Takeaways 120

Attribution 123

    Understanding attribution 123

    4 ways to do measurements 123

    How to measure geographic lift to test brand campaigns 124

Cross-channel attribution 125

First click, multi-click, and more 125

Working with Other Divisions **127**

Marketing 127

Tech 127

Sales 128

Legal 130

Campaigns in the Long Term **133**

Check what's working 133

Cohort vintage 133

What part is driving success? 134

Diminishing returns 134

Checklists for B2B Ad Performance **137**

B2B Ad Performance 137

Channel Check 137

All ad platforms 137

Paid Search 138

Paid Social 142

Reading Your B2B Ad Data **145**

Understanding your B2B ads Data is half the battle 145

Resources & Extras **147**

Making sense of buzzwords 147

Brand-building with B2B ads 149

Be cautious with influencers 151

How to be your agency's favorite client 151

The morality of B2B advertising 152

The future of B2B advertising 153

Cut through the noise with Right Percent 154

Right Percent stands out for three key reasons 155

Foreword

In 2016, I set out to find the very best marketers. Not the ones who got lucky or just grabbed a seat on a rocketship. I'm talking about the ones who were responsible for shifting the growth curve for their companies steeper, significantly and quickly, in ways others could not. Of course, doing so in one context with one set of tools does not ensure success in another context with a different set of tools. Predicting someone will be a star in a new role must consider both context and tools, including company stage and industry, business model, go-to-market strategy, marketing maturity, channel mix, and tech stack.

When I started out, I had no idea that my team and I would ultimately interview over 10,000 marketers and deploy over 2,000 marketers on projects based on their unique skillsets. I've seen the best, and the worst, and everything in between.

I was first introduced to Kevin after I sent an email to a marketing VP and asked, "I have a favor to ask—who are the best growth marketers you know?" Kevin was the only name he sent back. When I interviewed Kevin, he discussed his craft—B2B advertising—with naked enthusiasm and curiosity. It was clear he didn't practice it as much as he studied it. Like a child patiently pulling apart a toy to understand how it works, Kevin had already spent the better part of 6 years pulling apart the variables of advertising to understand how to make a channel sing. That is to say, to understand how to put in $1 and get back $2.

One of the primary lessons I've learned is that great *marketing* comes from great *marketers*. A great marketer isn't just a smart person that understands mechanics. Great marketers have a strong sense of ownership, a deconstructionist curiosity, and a tenacity that's powered by some combination of genuine interest in the subject matter and an internal loathing for unsolved puzzles. Kevin has all of these characteristics and has used his gifts to help company after company accelerate their growth, something I've witnessed firsthand.

Some may wonder whether designating this book "The B2B Ads Handbook" is a necessary differentiation from a B2C ads handbook. A decade ago, I was in this camp even after running performance marketing for Eventbrite, where my job was to acquire event organizers. I thought the magic was in understanding the channel mechanics, not their application to unique business models. I was dead wrong. Though the fundamental levers between B2C and B2B contexts are the same, the ways they are used are quite different. This results from different dynamics: longer sales cycles (and therefore more nurturing required), more customer stakeholders, non-sale conversion events (e.g. a demo), and higher AOVs and LTVs.

There's no shortage of marketers selling their formulas for success. And yet in my experience, they so rarely work. This is usually not because there's no truth in their strategies. Rather, it's because the success was context-dependent and the formulas, in an effort to be simple and pithy, offered very little of the underlying knowledge and synthesis that caused the "playbook" to be successful in the first place.

I hope you will find this book, as I have, to be beneficial both in the breadth of knowledge Kevin shares and in demonstrating how to synthesize that knowledge into actionable tactics and strategies in a B2B context. Do What Works will serve as a very handy reference manual as you deconstruct the growth challenges your company faces, in hopes of reconstructing your strategies and team to be smarter, better, and more effective.

Tyler Elliston
CEO & Founder
Right Side Up

How to Use This Book

What you'll learn

Over the last 6 years, my team at Right Percent has managed over $150 million in performance-driven B2B ad spend for companies like DoorDash, Ramp, Rippling, Brightwheel, Reddit and more.

This means we architected and executed campaigns, developed strategy, designed many thousands of ads, and had to report on performance and attribution throughout it all. For a few of these companies, we basically built out B2B ads from scratch all the way to IPO.

As we get into the levers of B2B ads and the practical side of this book, you're going to learn the same B2B best practices that top companies use, directly from the team who invented many of these ideas and methodologies.

What you'll achieve

On average, Right Percent's clients see about a 46% improvement in ROI after they start with us, while also more than doubling ad spend. In theory, if you follow these practices to a 't', you should be able to realize significant improvement in your ROI. Realistically, if you follow everything in this book and re-do your campaigns to align with these principles and methods, you're going to make your campaigns perform 10 to 40% better.

This book is your portable B2B ads agency.

How Ads Fit Into Marketing Strategy

Most B2B companies did not grow from scratch with ads as their primary channel. They typically got where they are through the founder's personal network, outbound sales, or some other difficult-to-scale channel. By the time they branch out into ads, they ideally have a few dozen (or several hundred) customers and have already established product-market fit. Which, of course, might sound like a good place to be, and it is. But without an effective strategy and a functional knowledge of how to spend that budget well, these businesses won't get the most out of ads, and they may even end up getting in their own way when trying to work with outside experts like ad agencies.

Why ads matter more than ever

"Do ads still matter in 2025?" is the kind of clickbait hot-take I want to help readers avoid. But it is worth unpacking to illustrate some key points about the value of ads and why, in spite of everything ads can do for your business, they are often overlooked. The truth is ads never stopped mattering.

For the purposes of this book and any takeaways on the merits of B2B advertising, we're talking about high-budget, ROI-positive campaigns that have trackable outcomes.

The tracking component is what makes ads more powerful than ever. The first major strength of ads is the way they enable quick learning. Done right, you can gather major insights in a month or two. Almost no other channel lets you do that.

Other channels all have pros and cons compared to ads:

- SEO, by comparison, is a glacial game . . . and like a glacier, your successes can melt away with abrupt fluctuations in the search engine climate.
- Cold email is becoming harder and harder over time as AI spam volume has skyrocketed, and spam filters have been improved.
- Event marketing can be very successful but is hard to scale (and can be supported by ads).
- Direct mail costs at least $75k to do a minimum test and only works in certain situations.
- Posting on organic social (LinkedIn, Instagram, etc.) is a good long-term strategy, but has few good feedback loops and takes a long time and effort to drive pipeline.

Ads, by contrast, deliver a unique feedback loop in which you spend money to reach your target audience, learning in the process how to refine your approach to get in front of more qualified people.

The other big strength of ads is scalability. If an ad works and you spend $10,000 and it does really well, you can spend $100,000 and have it do really *really* well. Most things get harder as they scale. You want to scale your outbound sales team? That means hiring and training more salespeople and incurring those costs. Want to do more SEO? You have to write a hundred more articles to move the needle. With ads, it's possible to 10x your spend for 10x results.

Potential B2B Ad Outcomes

"But we're already running ads . . . "

Most companies do run ads at some level or try to. It's rare to find a B2B company with real customers and real revenue that's not running ads to some extent. But those ads rarely live up to their potential. And by potential, I don't mean it in some abstract way, I mean it in terms of well-defined metrics. A fully optimized B2B company can see something like 50% of new revenue originating from ads. By contrast, the average B2B company might realize around 10% of new revenue from their ads (and might think that's all that's possible from the channel).

One reason a company might not be fully optimized is that the skill required is very rare. It's not bragging, just a statement of fact, to say that our team is made up of some of the very few people on the planet who have scaled a B2B ad account past $500,000 or more a month. That means the average company is going to have a hard time finding and retaining talent, especially because it's so specialized. You might have someone who's great on LinkedIn but doesn't know Facebook or search. One of the main value propositions of a team-for-hire like Right Percent is that we have senior players who've done this all before. But using this book should get any team closer to getting optimal performance from their B2B ads.

One piece of the puzzle

Another thing that makes ads tricky is that they're just one piece of a greater puzzle. An ad leads people to your funnel, but you need to close those leads, usually with a sales team, a product-led growth flow, or any number of other elements of the funnel. For instance, the offer you use to entice people to click your ad has a huge impact on how successful your campaign can be. Your offer could be just a demo with your sales team, a great free content template, or even a gift card for qualified prospects. If that or any other piece of the puzzle isn't in place, the ad itself is not going to work. You need that whole flow, of which ads are just the beginning. We'll go over all the levers that matter later in this book.

Additive

Using advertising to drive demand from new audiences is mostly additive (no pun intended). We're not taking away from any other channel, we're introducing a new source of scalable growth, which can come from ads. So, in a way, indexing strongly on ads actually increases your channel and revenue diversification. It's another tool to help you ramp acquisition up or down, making it a useful lever for finance teams to have.

Need growth? Increase ads (once you're optimized, that is).

Need to save money? Reduce spend to your most marginally effective ads.

Strategic Takeaways

- Ads have the unique advantage of being able to scale quickly and flexibly.
- Ads offer a reliable path to growth amid the uncertainty and long-term nature of many other ad channels.

B2B Advertising 101

Advertising vs. marketing vs. sales

Since these terms are going to come up a lot and, in some cases, be used interchangeably, we might as well define them and clarify how they're different and where they overlap.

Marketing

Marketing is a higher-level concept than advertising. It's everything that you're doing to take your product to market. It's all the work that goes into the process of connecting companies with customers. Broadly speaking, acquiring customers is the bulk of what marketing's job is: That's things like SEO, email, and setting up a booth at conferences. All the things that put the product in front of customers that's not a direct sales touch.

Nurturing is another important function of marketing that touches everything from drip campaigns to UX and website functionality. We're not just responsible for bringing leads in the door, but holding their hands until they close into customers (and often beyond).

Marketing operations are all the behind-the-scenes work to make sure all the pieces connect, that leads are acquired and nurtured, and that all of this information is tracked so marketers can make effective decisions.

Advertising

Advertising is a small subsection of marketing where you pay to get in front of potential customers. While advertising is only a section of marketing, it is the subject of this book.

The main advantages of advertising, from a marketing perspective, is the ability to do quick tests and get results faster than any other channel. The other thing advertising does well is scalability. The faster you test, the sooner you know where to put your money, and the more money you can make from a campaign. If you have $10,000 you can use it to run tests that will tell you, with reasonable accuracy, where to spend your next $100,000 profitably.

For B2B marketing managers, ads are one tool, one lever in your toolbox designed to help you test and promote your product. It's a powerful lever, it's an expensive one, and not one to be used all the time.

Here's some quick guidelines on when ads are a good fit for your B2B company

- You already have product-market fit. This means you know customers want to pay money for your product and you ideally have at least 50 paying customers. Ads are often too expensive to use before you've figured out your product-market fit.
- You have the ability to track leads down your funnel all the way to when they become customers, at least 70% of the time. If you can't track what happens to leads after they come in, you can't run a successful ad campaign.
- You have the means to close customers (either through a sales team or a product designed for onboarding).
- You're comfortable testing with at least $10,000, ideally $20,000, to prove out an ad channel. If that number makes you gasp, you're probably too early to test ads. Like I said earlier, it's an expensive road. But you will learn in months instead of years what works.

> *People often talk about two branches of advertising: Brand and Direct Response. Brand usually refers to large-scale campaigns without clear acquisition-related goals (like leads), as opposed to Direct Response, which is 100% focused on ads leading to trackable outcomes.*
>
> *Brand and direct response are often distinct siloes within companies, often delineating very different career paths for advertisers in those siloes. They use different languages and different metrics for success.*

> *In my mind, these branches are much more similar than different and are siloed unnecessarily. It's more a matter of measurement differences than anything else. But more on that later in this book.*

The age of iteration

Old school advertising was brutal. Then, as now, money would talk, but you would have to wait for it to finish before you could listen. In TV advertising, direct mail, and other print media, you would plan like crazy, dot every "i" and cross every "t" before finally sending your ad out into the world. Then it was time to pray, because if that commercial goes out in the world and it bombs, you flushed a year's worth of budget and ad spend down the drain.

Today's iterative approach to digital advertising is much more forgiving. We have the luxury of learning incrementally from what works and what doesn't without having to bet the farm on any one headline. We get to play and try things on for size. Ask anyone working in ads today and I'm sure they'll agree that this is the more comfortable dynamic to work in. The irony is that the old school marketers of yore would struggle with the modern, iterative style. The old way required meticulous planning and getting it right on paper first, which is a terrible approach for a modern campaign because it leaves no room for learning and feedback.

So, rather than awe clients with an impressive pitch and flawless design, I tell them we're going to make twenty ads over a few months. I advise them not to overthink creative and not to go back and forth on any particular ad. Don't quibble over the copy. Of course, we should QA for typos and make sure everything is on brand, but it's better just to cut ads from the list we're not sure of than spend a lot of time editing them.

It doesn't need to be perfect, because unlike in traditional ads, *hardly anyone is going to see it*. Of the 20 or so ads we run, 19 or so will reach a double-digit audience before the algorithm decides they're not good enough. And then one ad is going to get all the spend. That's the power law of modern digital advertising. You are rewarded by iterating, creating a lot of stuff and seeing what works. It's not about the perfect tagline or memorable slogan, it's about writing a lot of different positioning statements and seeing which one does best. Companies trying to do new advertising the old way, where everything goes through nine layers of approval and countless drafts, end up frustrated because they're going to lose against people who don't have the same friction.

The new way is flexible and scalable. The iterative approach lets you know your decisions as an advertiser or CMO actually have a substantial business impact. Another, deeper thing to like about this methodology is it reveals the truth about the world and about the market. People can tell you all sorts of things about their values, preferences, etc. But their clicks and their dollars never lie.

B2B vs. B2C

B2B audience sizes are almost universally smaller than B2C, and this changes a lot about what marketing tactics work. Here's an example:

B2C sells T-shirts.

B2B sells T-shirt printing machines.

The difference between these products and their customers influences how you advertise them in so many ways. You can probably imagine an ad for a T-shirt. It's going to show someone wearing the T-shirt, and it's going to focus more on grabbing attention than speaking to intent. On the other hand, I doubt you have a visual in your head for what an ad for a t-shirt machine might look like. But the strategy for advertising one would probably be more about the utility it offers and how it out-performs alternatives.

The main variable changing between selling t-shirts and t-shirt printing machines is *audience size*. There are way more people in the market for t-shirts (you're probably wearing one) than there are T-shirt factory stakeholders. So, the B2B ad almost always addresses a smaller target audience.

Qualification is another way of looking at this key factor. In B2C, you only need a customer to have intent since anyone can buy the product. In B2B, you need qualification *and* intent. Only someone with a t-shirt business could buy the printing machine. Qualification can be made up of many factors, such as the size of the company you're targeting or the title of the person within that company.

We'll get way deeper into this in the sections on audience and creative.

Strategic Takeaways

- B2B advertising is generally utilitarian. It's about offering a solution to your customer's problem.
- Modern B2B advertising is iterative. Forget about the perfect headline, run tests and see what works.
- One of the core differences between B2B and B2C ads is that qualification is much more important in B2B.

The Levers of B2B Advertising

In advertising, as in life, you're better off focusing on what you can control. The levers of B2B ads are the only variables you can influence to affect a result from an ad account. Anything you do to get results fits into one of these buckets. So, if you imagine yourself as the operator of a marketing machine, these are the levers you can pull. To master the levers of B2B advertising is to learn a strategic skillset that will make you more effective at your job and will help drive revenue for your company.

When should you invest more in audience lists to target vs relying on platform algorithms? That's the kind of strategic thinking we want to help you internalize. By understanding the levers and how to use them, you gain a high-level understanding of strategy grounded in the fundamentals of how *B2B advertising works*.

The Four Levers of B2B Advertising

The levers you have when running B2B ads are audience, offer, conversion event, and creative/copy. We will have a short description of each here, and a whole segment covering each lever in the coming pages.

What four **levers** do B2B marketing leaders have to beat **paid media goals**?

Test different **audiences** and/or keywords.

Test different **offers** and experiences in your ads.

Systematize making **ad creative and copy**.

Test new **conversion events** to optimize on.

Audience is essentially deciding where your ads show up. On LinkedIn, this can be an audience based on job titles. On Facebook, this can be determined through their proprietary algorithm that creates a profile of their users. On Search, this is the keywords you choose to show up for.

Offer is what the user gets by clicking on your ad. The offer could be a landing page, a piece of content, an incentive, or whatever you're promoting. The important thing is to think carefully about what you want to promote and why you think it will be effective. Your offer is not something you tack on after the fact—it should be part of your initial plan. There will be a full chapter on offers later on.

Conversion event is what you're measuring as the result of users clicking the ad. It's also about being clear about what you're looking for as a leading indicator of a campaign success. What do you want to learn from your first test? What's the goal? Is it leads, demo sets, or something else? Are only leads with over 100 employees valuable to you? Do they have to have certain titles? What kind of lead is most likely to convert to a customer 90 days from now? Determining this before your campaign starts is very important.

Usually, you'll want to set up these qualifying lead events within the ad platforms to optimize on them from the start.

Creative is what your ad says and looks like. The most important aspect is positioning—finding several different ways to position your offer to optimize for a leading indicator conversion event.

With these levers, the outcome you're always solving for is eventual revenue and profits. For every dollar you spend on ads, you want to gain more than that on your bottom line. The levers are how you make your ad dollars more efficient.

Lever 1—Audience: Targeting Your Target Market

Who is the person who can make the decision to buy your product? That person is your "target market." When you're making your ad strategy, the target market is not just the amount or size of the companies that can use your product, but *the number of decision-makers who can make the decision to buy your product*. This is because decision-makers are the people who will actually click and convert from your ads.

In some industries, there are millions of potential decision-makers who could decide to buy your product. In others, there might only be 5,000 applicable decision-makers in the world. See the chart below. It shows one way to look at which of the three main ad channels (plus TikTok) to use in any situation.

B2B audience size impacts
channel ad strategy

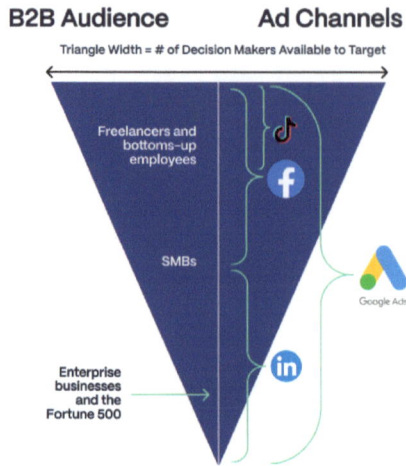

Let's look at the example of going after enterprise.

If you have a top-down approach, it means you have a small target market because there's only around 10,000 C-suite executives in *Fortune* 500 companies who can make the decision to use your product. That is your target market: the decision-makers in their companies, not the companies themselves. Make no mistake, you're in the people-based marketing game, specifically, those exact people. Anyone else on the planet is a waste of your time and resources.

Now, let's imagine a different approach. Instead of targeting the CIO or whoever, you go bottoms up and go after any engineer at the company with an offer to try out your product. If they like it, they can try to push it to their product team. A lot of Product-Led-Growth (PLG) companies start that way. Even though you would be going after the same companies, your strategy will be completely different, because instead of 10,000 or so people, you're targeting millions who work at these companies.

It works the same way when you're targeting small businesses. It's easier to reach them via Facebook than it is to reach the heads of big corporations because there are more of them who can make the decision. Every small business owner is a decision-maker. Many of them are the *only* decision-makers in their company.

So, ultimately, B2B is a kind of misleading term because your real target will always be anyone who can make a decision to buy your product. Focus on the decision-makers.

Channel ends up being so important that it's worth considering simultaneously with the development of your offer, or even *before* in some cases. For example, if your audience and goal considerations tell you that you're looking for high-intent users, Google is probably your channel, and that will dictate what kind of offer works best.

To help you figure out which channel will work best, let's take a quick look at the three main B2B ad channels. We'll get into channel-specific guides in a later section, but here's what you need to know about the strengths and weaknesses of each channel, and how they relate to target audience.

Google

Google can work across any amount of decision-makers. It works if you're targeting enterprise, micro-B, or SMB. But Google needs intent to make the engine run. So, people must already know your product exists and be searching for it.

Something to keep in mind is that Google puts you in direct competition with other people. So, for instance, if you're selling business loans, that's a very competitive vertical. LendingTree, NerdWallet, Ondeck, and their smaller competitors are all appearing together at the same time. This is the main drawback of a non-brand keyword. Searchers for that term aren't just seeing you, they're seeing your competitors. Which is great if you're a top result, but frustrating and costly if you're not. Search is very competitive, and if you can't make enough money per customer, you're going to lose auctions. For example, if Lending Tree makes $100 per customer that comes in from search and Capita makes $50, Capita can't afford the bids to stay on the same page. In other words, it pays to be a winner.

Social

There's a lot more to say about social, but for now, to compare it with search, the advantage is you can reach your customers one-on-one, rather than alongside competing offers, and you can reach folks who don't have intent yet. Facebook and LinkedIn scrollers are not necessarily looking for you and your offer, which means you need to do more work to grab their interest.

The 3 Ad Platform Targeting Strategies

The number of decision-makers does not only affect channel strategy, but also targeting type strategy.

There are three types of targeting, as I've briefly mentioned before.

- Manual
- List-Based
- Algorithmic

Each is useful in different circumstances, and it's important to know when to use each.

Which platforms are best suited for each type of targeting (in order of effectiveness)?

Google AdWords	Linked in ads	facebook Ads
1. Manual Targeting (keywords)	1. Manual Targeting (job history)	1. Algorithmic Targeting
2. Algorithmic Targeting	2. List based targeting	2. List based targeting
3. List Based targeting	3. Algorithmic Targeting	3. Manual targeting (interests)

Manual Man

Manual targeting means fiddling with the platform. If you're checking boxes, selecting drop-downs, and moving sliders, you're manually targeting. On LinkedIn this could be selecting industry, seniority, or company.

In search, this is keyword selection and some interest group layering. Manual targeting can get super tactical and even a little nasty. In B2B, you're always looking for qualification, and on Google, this means qualified clicks. In a technical use case, a Salesforce user could be immediately qualified for your Salesforce integration. Another type of manual targeting via search is brand bidding, where you bid on your own name. Whereas competitor bidding, you bid on your competitor's name. Brutal, but often effective.

On Facebook, it's selecting interest groups like "small business owner." But manual targeting is generally ineffective on Facebook. We'll get into why that is later.

LinkedIn, the master of manual

LinkedIn reigns supreme in manual targeting. List-based is successful on LinkedIn as well, especially for enterprise-focused, smaller, decision-maker audiences. Their algorithmic targeting leaves a lot to be desired, however.

The real strength of LinkedIn is if you can pick manual targets that are very precise and backed by good data and target them. It's also a great place to split things up into verticals. Manual bidding works well and goes hand-in-hand with manual targeting on LinkedIn.

On Google, if you bid $9 and your nearest competitor bids $8, Google will charge you $8.01 to win the auction. On LinkedIn, if you make the winning bid with $9, LinkedIn charges you $9. So, with manual targeting on LinkedIn, you need to adjust your bids manually to get the most effective outcome.

LinkedIn wants to become more algorithmic over time, and it's constantly rolling out new products to that end. It's not there yet, but keep your eyes peeled.

List-based targeting

Also known as third-party and first-party targeting, this is where you have a list of thousands of prospects or leads. You upload them to platforms and target them that way. It's as simple as it sounds. There are a range of CRM and audience building tools to help with varying levels of complexity. For instance, tools like 6Sense or ZoomInfo can populate for you to target in ad platforms. Lists are how you generally build out one-to-one and one-to-few targeting in an Account-Based Marketing (ABM) strategy.

Algorithmic targeting

This type of targeting is all about the conversion signal.

All modern ad platforms, such as Meta, Google and LinkedIn, allow you to optimize for conversion events. A conversion event can be set on anything the user does – clicking a button, getting to a certain page, or filling out a form.

The conversion event that you choose "trains" the ad platform to bring you the kind of users you want. For instance, if you optimize on just users filling out a simple lead form that only asks for email address, Facebook will say "no problem, boss" and go out and get you plenty of leads. But they'll be the cheapest leads who generally won't convert into customers.

A good example of this dynamic is in the small business lending vertical. If you optimize on users filling out a simple lead form, you will get many applicants for business loans who won't qualify for them. But if you set your conversion event at the part of your funnel when the user uploads their bank documents, for instance, it will train the ad algorithm to find more users who look and act similarly to those higher-quality users. See example below.

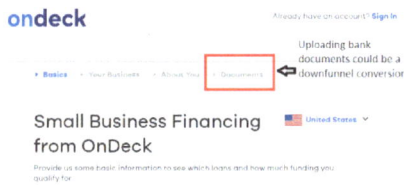

Facebook in particular is so good at algorithmic targeting, that for most clients we use "broad" baseline targeting where our ad campaigns are set to reach everyone in the USA. With broad targeting in place, we rely on a mix of our conversion signal and creative to find customers for our clients to great success. Algorithmic targeting is Facebook's bread and butter, and that's 90% of what we do on that platform, but they're also decent at list-based targeting. If you have a list, you can upload it to Facebook and use it to reach them. But forget about manual B2B targeting on Facebook (more on that later).

Google, a hybrid . . . sort of

Google is an interesting one because it's primarily powered by manual targeting, like picking the right keywords for your industry and client needs. But its algorithmic capabilities have come a long way. It was terrible five years ago. Nowadays, like on Facebook, you can run a very broad-reaching keyword campaign and still find success if you have a high-quality conversion event.

In general, conversion events are very important on Google, but you still need to do the legwork of manual and intensive keyword research. Many effective AdWords accounts that we run use exclusively manual, exact match targeting with limited reliance on algorithmic targeting.

Data and list-based targeting are almost non-existent on Google Search for various reasons. The biggest reason is that no matter what list you upload, there's no guarantee they're searching for any of your keywords.

You can use list-based targeting on Google's other more attention-based platforms, such as YouTube or Google Display Network. However, these placements generally perform worse than LinkedIn or Facebook, so we don't recommend this until you've thoroughly explored those channels.

The Three Main B2B Audience Segments

Now that you know the fundamentals of B2B audience strategy, let's get into how to approach each of the main B2B segments.

These are the general category rules, though there are exceptions in every direction.

Enterprise—Under 50k decision-makers
SMB: 50k – 5 million decision-makers
B2MicroB: 5 million+ decision-makers

Targeting Enterprise Audiences (Traditional B2B)

How big is big? How small is too small?

My rule of thumb is that if you have over 200,000 decision-makers who can buy your product, that's big for a B2B audience. Algorithmic channels like Meta can work great for you with that audience size.

Under 200,000, you should lean towards LinkedIn, and under 50,000 you can forget about Facebook, and just focus on LinkedIn down to an audience of around 5,000. If your audience is under 5,000, ads won't really work for you. You can run some ads to assist your sales team at that audience size, and you can always set up retargeting ads, but ads will never be a major channel for you because, ultimately, ads are a medium of mass communication, while smaller audiences are sales and relationship driven.

Bad news first

When targeting enterprise companies, you're usually targeting a smaller audience of under 50,000 people. Because of this, you will have fewer conversions such as leads and opportunities on a weekly and monthly basis. This hurts you in many ways. For one, your own team has a harder time learning which campaigns are working.

It can make it really hard to tell when you have statistically significant results.

If there are five conversions in one campaign and ten in the next, that's twice as many, but is it statistically significant? You can use ChatGPT to help you.

ChatGPT to the rescue

Statistical significance used to be the bane of marketing organizations because marketers, as a rule, don't know math. But now ChatGPT can handle your stats with amazing results.

For example, one campaign may have 20 conversions with a $10,000 spend, while another has 27 conversions with the same spend. AI can do a whole statistical test for you with incredible accuracy.

What's really cool about this use of AI is that it's just plain language. It's not math. You just ask it what you want to know, feed it the numbers you have, and it gets to work.

If I spend $10,000 in ad spend in Campaign A and get 27 conversions, and $10,000 spend in Campaign B and get 20 conversions, do I know that campaign A did better than campaign B?

Conclusion:

While Campaign A has more conversions, the difference **is not statistically significant**. The results could be due to chance, so you should **not yet assume A is truly better than B** without more data. [>-]

How many more conversions would campaign A need than campaign B to be stat sig?

Campaign A would need **5 additional conversions** (for a total of **32 conversions**) to reach statistical significance compared to Campaign B, assuming the same $10,000 spend for both.

At **32 conversions vs. 20**, the difference would likely be statistically significant at $p < 0.05$. [>-]

So why bother with enterprise?

Simply put, because enterprise is where the money is in B2B SaaS. Somewhere around 90% of the market capitalization in the S&P 500 falls into this category. So, if you're sleeping on enterprise, you're missing out. It's a smaller audience, it's hard to target, but man, oh man, is it lucrative.

How to target smaller audiences on Enterprise and Mid-Market

Audience size greatly impacts your targeting strategy. In the below diagram, you can see as the triangle width (which represents the size of your target audience) gets smaller, the most effective targeting technique changes.

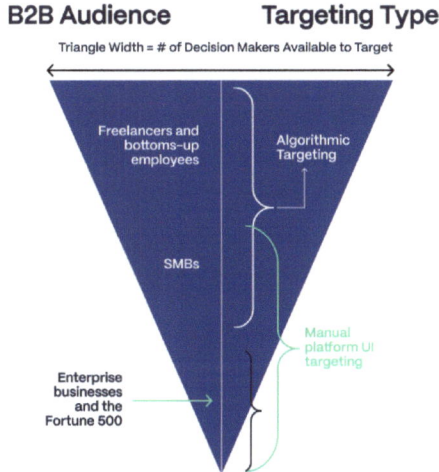

The first way is **manual platform UI targeting**. This is what works for companies that can spend hundreds of thousands per month using manual targeting on LinkedIn with hyper accuracy. Think of the meme of the girl who's "looking for a man in finance . . . " For example,

- People in the finance industry
- With under 100 employees

It can be much more complex than that. See below for a sample audience that works well for a B2B ads company.

And other factors you can control on LinkedIn. With those parameters, you can successfully target a mix of mid-market and enterprise companies. This approach is great because it lets you land big and small customers or, "eat all parts of the buffalo" as I often advise our clients.

You want to monetize as many possible types of leads as you can because it makes your advertising more efficient. If the audience is too small to the point where manual targeting won't work, then you want to use list-based ABM. This means, assuming you have a sales team, that the sales team has a list of target accounts they're pursuing. You just upload that list to LinkedIn, or Facebook, or wherever and target them there by way of supporting your sales team.

Clicks, good and bad

As we've discussed, enterprise audiences are small. That means you don't have as much data. When trying to fix this, the big mistake people make is optimizing for clicks. The thinking is, "Oh well, if we can't get 30 conversions per week, let's just optimize on getting 'em to click. We can handle hundreds of clicks."

But unless you're doing that methodically and are careful about who you're serving, it's a terrible metric because a click doesn't mean much. There are just too many bad clicks. And, so, the campaign never learns who's a good customer and who's a waste of time.

As a rule, you should never be running a click campaign unless you already know all this and have a genuine understanding of why click campaigns are a bad idea, and why the one you're running is an exception.

The exception that proves the rule

Here's one such scenario. You have a really tight, proven audience, like we talked about in relation to brand campaigns. You're applying the "Create L.I.F.E" principle and using a product strategy with full market coverage and building a rock solid first or third-party data audience.

If that all sounds like gibberish, don't even think about running a click campaign.

ABM

We've mentioned ABM, Account-Based Marketing, before, but it's worth unpacking it here to underscore some subtle differences in the approach to SaaS. LinkedIn advertising is a natural channel for ABM because more than 750 million professionals are on LinkedIn, and their targeting allows you to reach them with uploaded lists. Best of all, it allows you to reach prospects when they're in a business mindset.

3 kinds of ABM

There are three ways to do ABM targeting.

One-to-Many—You take your whole list of accounts, say 20,000 accounts, and you target them all with the same ad or group of ads. This can work because you're working from a proven list.

One-to-few—You split that many into smaller lists. So, from 20,000 names, you'll do 5,000 in your B2B gaming, 5,000 in SaaS, 5,000 in education, etc. and you target each of those with its own ads on LinkedIn. This approach tends to work well, and it's something I recommend frequently. Any ad that makes someone say, "this ad is just for me" is bound to be effective.

One-to-one—Now, you can go even further with a one-to-one ABM. This is what a lot of people imagine when they think ABM. Let's say you have a campaign targeting executives at The GAP. They'll see your ad and go, "GAP executive, that's me!" The only problem with that approach is you have to be a big company to pull this off, and you need a dialed-in sales team going after the same thing because conversion issues and account issues get amplified 10,000-fold with this strategy.

Most B2B SaaS companies in an early stage are better served by going with the many-to-few model, where you focus on targeting entire verticals like Finance or Retail, as opposed to targeting individual companies. With this approach, you get a lot more data and not that much loss of conversion events. On top of that, it requires much less effort than creating separate campaigns for everything and trying to find an approach that works for everyone across the board. Otherwise, you'd have to handle extensive backend work, like setting up individualized email flows for each company

Many-to-few is the go-to model until you get big enough and mature enough that you can graduate to many-to-one or few-to-one. And even then, I would do so carefully.

Going Deeper into ABM

Nowadays (in 2025), ABM tools have advanced even further, with some platforms like 6Sense offering powerful intent signals. We've had many clients use audiences from these platforms to successfully target users on Facebook and LinkedIn.

The important thing to remember is that advertising is a small portion of your ABM strategy. The strategy starts with the sales team—they must determine a list and a sales strategy for going after these accounts. Sales figures out which data provider is the best fit for their target market. Then, marketing can support sales in several ways. One way is designing email campaigns to accompany the sales offers. Another is designing custom content for these ABM lists. Lastly, there are ads.

It is rarely worth a marketing team paying for 6Sense or similar tools on their own, since targeting lists without sales support rarely generates enough ROI to be worth it.

ABM Ads Supporting Sales—Best Practices

You want to upload the available list the sales team is using to the appropriate ad platforms. Usually this is LinkedIn to start, since it's most effective, and then other platforms after you're confident the campaign is helping.

All list-based audiences exhaust quickly as people on the list are quickly shown your ads. Therefore, you need at least 6 distinct offers to display for the users in your target list.

This can include:

Ungated content—Just a link to something on your website with no email gate. Industry case studies are great for this.

Thought leadership—This is a LinkedIn ad unit with just text from a personal account. Most effective from C-Suite with fleshed out profiles and a good profile picture.

Gated content—We talk about gated content a lot in this book, but make sure to include templates and checklists.

Webinar invitations, in-person invitations, and any other live events you have—Live events are like sales calls.

Incentives—Offering people free branded swag or conference tickets can be very effective. Another effective incentive is the buyout, where you offer to buy out a competitor's remaining contract months if the client switches to your product.

Should you gate content?

Gating content means requiring prospects to give you their contact information to receive the asset. Most of the time, you should promote gated content vs ungated content in your ads for the following reasons:

- People do convert into paying customers at scale from gated content. It's a tried and true strategy.
- Without gating content, it is very hard to get attribution and figure out which content campaigns are driving performance. This means campaigns can't iterate and improve over time from learnings, which is key to long-term performance.

The exception to this is for very small, proven audiences, especially for ABM. If you have a precise list the sales team is already reaching, you can serve ungated content as part of the overall marketing effort. You can test the impact of this ungated spend with a geographic or list-based split test.

Measuring ABM Ads

As you can imagine, these campaigns can't be measured the way normal B2B performance campaigns are, since not every offer is trackable. There are two ways to track performance.

One is qualitative and holistic—how many people are visiting your pages? How many people are downloading the gated content? Are you getting engagement on posts? Does the sales team say people are remembering or mentioning your ads?

The other is quantitative but usually requires at least $75k in budget. When you start your campaign, you randomly split your list of accounts to target in half. One-half gets the whole ad treatment above, and the other gets nothing.

Did one side of the test respond to more sales emails? Your CRM will determine what data you have, but there's almost always some kind of metric you can measure lift on. You generally need at least $75k in ad spend for this since you want plenty of data on both sides of the test if you want to see statistical significance.

Channel for enterprise

The two channels that work best for enterprise targeting (going after large companies with at least 1,000 employees) are Google and LinkedIn. Everything else is a very distant competitor to these two.

Google works for everybody if they have intent. It spans a wide spectrum, which is why Google prints money.

If you don't have an intent-based market, let's say you're inventing a new category like underwear apps that nobody is searching for, then you'll need to focus on attention-based advertising, which, for the audience sizes in enterprise, means LinkedIn.

Sales > marketing

Another key difference for B2Enterprise is that the sales team is much more important than the marketing team. The smaller your audience gets, the more important the sales team becomes. So, for instance, if you have an audience of 500,000, the sales team is kind of interchangeable. Marketing generates leads, sales closes them, and sales doesn't have much to do with strategy, they're just part of your funnel.

In enterprise-focused efforts with bigger deal sizes, the sales team is much more important. It's marketing's job to support sales. Sales takes the lead in strategy, and marketing just figures out how to give them what they need.

In B2Enterprise, the lines between prospecting and retargeting are blurred. If you have a sales cycle that's six to twelve months long, the difference between someone clicking on your ads that are targeted towards a list or targeted towards a select group on LinkedIn and people who have already seen your stuff is blurry. Over the course of several months to years, people will frequently click on both. So, in practice, you end up combining prospecting and retargeting all the time. In B2SMB, by contrast, they're usually cleanly separated because retargeting happens after a lot of people close right away from the first click and first conversion.

Measure what you can manage

Cohort analysis is important. You never want to measure your down-funnel results, like closed deals, from the day they close. If you close 100 deals in December, they likely originated from all sorts of deals and conversions throughout the year. Just knowing that the deal closed in December doesn't help you in your ad account management at all, because the whole purpose of tracking results is to tell you how you can change your campaigns to get better data.

You need to compare apples to apples.

If you're looking at April data, you should look at leads that originated in April, whenever they eventually closed. If they close in May, add them to your April data. If they close next September, add 'em to April. This is what I mean when I say cohort data is so important because the lead-created date is the part you impacted in marketing. The close date was the sales team. You had little to do with that timing. You need to measure the part you have the power to make decisions over.

Offer for enterprise

In our section on offer, we get into the appeal of reports and studies for enterprise audiences. There's a social-proof element to reports with data from Deloitte or McKinsey, but there's also an element of peer pressure at work with offers like these. Enterprise decision-makers care a lot about being on the right side of trends and having the deniability that comes with following prevailing wisdom. This makes sense, given that risky decisions can put their job on the line in a way safe bets don't. Therefore, it helps to have an offer that puts their mind at ease and lets them know they're making the right decision.

Creative best practices for enterprise

Some creative rules (that we'll get into in much more detail in the section on creative) remain constant across B2B ads. You want big visual headlines, etc. Where there's a big difference in B2Enterprise, especially if you're going top-down: VPs and other leaders won't try your demo. They don't have time, they're not technical, and they don't care. They're just not going to have any interest in getting under the hood of a demo to poke around and see if your product is right for their business.

Generally speaking, content advertising is more effective for more senior people. With any luck, they'll read it and pass it around to their team. Considering how busy they are, it has to be quick and digestible, high credibility, and value-added. They tend to trust people in high positions like they are. Take this book, for example. It probably means more to a C-suite exec coming from a fellow business leader than if it had been written by a copywriter. No offense to copywriters.

Social proof is a much more important ingredient of content with enterprise than it would be for SMB. Small business owners don't care who you are if your template looks useful. They'll download the jankiest-looking spreadsheet if it helps them do their job. But the reason Enterprise wants Gartner reports and anything from Deloitte, McKinsey, and the *Harvard Business Review*, is they're much more risk-averse. Keep this in mind with regards to the subject of your case studies, if you're using those as part of your content offer. The more name recognition the better.

To recap the golden rules of creative for advertising to enterprise:

Focus on content

Demonstrate that you're appealing, safe, and will make them look good.

Targeting Small Business Audiences (B2SMB)

AKA 1/5th of the American workforce . . .

There are many ways to define B2SMB, but let's start by distinguishing it from B2Micro-B. An SMB, in the broadest possible terms, is any business that has at least one employee. There are around 6 million such businesses in the United States, and if you expand the definition to include people who own their own businesses and have no employees, that number is closer to 40 million.

So, it's a big number and a big audience. The decision maker you're trying to reach is the owner of the business. Always. I've seen B2SMB campaigns try to go through the accountant or the lawyer, and it never works. An SMB owner might rely on those people for certain functions of their operations, but they don't trust those people to make real business decisions.

Your target is the owner, and they are very, very busy.

Nailing your SMB offer

Content and incentive offers work well. The best kind of content ads are brief and to the point. Dry, analytical, and for lack of a better word, boring, content that works with enterprise, like reports and white papers, won't get through here. SMB owners want templates, checklists, and things that are useful in day-to-day life they can get value right away. The challenge when crafting your offer is to find a way to connect the value of the offer to the value your company provides.

B2SMB has a faster sales cycle than enterprise, but leading indicators are still very important. No successful B2SMB company optimizes on just closed leads. You'll want to differentiate qualified ones.

Of the three types of targeting—manual, third-party, and algorithmic—algorithmic works best for B2SMB, especially on Facebook. The high number of decision-makers and faster close cycle mean you can train the algorithm to drive qualified leads.

B2SMB is a Facebook Game

Facebook is the undisputed king of SMB. Google also works because it works for anything, as long as you have intent. TikTok can work for B2Micro-B, but it hasn't cracked B2SMB yet, and its format, which caters to ludicrously short bursts of attention, has its limits for B2B use in general.

So, for B2SMB, you're looking at Facebook almost exclusively. Like Facebook users, SMB owners tend to be on the older side, 40 and up. If they're established, if they have revenue, they're older.

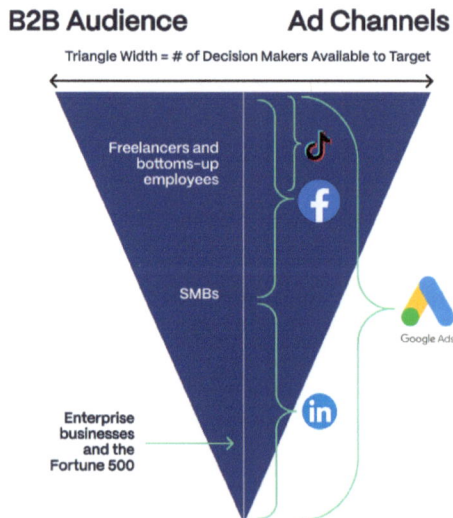

B2B audience size impacts channel ad strategy

Targeting Micro-Business Audiences (B2MicroB)

B2MicroB is a funny category. It's not what people think of when they think of B2B. On the surface, many of these appear to be consumer products marketed to individual consumers. However, what makes their approach to strategy closer to B2B than B2C is their emphasis on the utility of the product coupled with a goal of reaching highly qualified, high-intent audiences.

You don't actually need a lot of the leading indicators in B2MicroB because there are enough conversions that you can optimize for your end-goal conversions. For example, a financial services company could optimize for people making their first deposit. DoorDash can optimize for people becoming "Dashers." The creative principles remain the same, and you still want to use visual headlines.

Qualification remains vital. Even though there are more people in a B2MicroB target audience, not everybody is your target. You still need a solid conversion event and creative that speaks directly to your target audience.

Here are a few examples:

MasterClass

Masterclass sells premium online courses taught by the undisputed masters of their fields. Aaron Sorkin teaches screenwriting, and Annie Leibowitz teaches photography. They run subscription plans for something like $180 per year. While this appears to be a consumer product, their acquisition strategy focuses on the utility of up-skilling for "prosumer" high-level hobbyists and creative professionals like photographers and freelance writers.

This is a great example of B2MicroB where you use ads to target individual decision-makers. A channel like Meta is great in this use case.

Robo-Advisor Platforms for Investing

Another great example of B2MicroB are robo-advising platforms and other investing software. The value proposition of a robo-investing platform is bringing financial tools once reserved for the super-rich to everyday investors. You want to get people with high net worth to deposit money with your company. Like any B2B campaign, qualifying the leads that come in is very important. In the end, it's targeting individual decision-makers with a utilitarian motive.

Podia

This all-in-one platform for building websites and online courses focuses on its utility to influencers who need these assets to grow their solopreneur businesses. Targeting solopreneurs is a classic use case of B2MicroB advertising.

These and countless other B2MicroB cases illustrate the three key differentiators of B2B ads best practices vs. B2C:

Qualification—Are these exactly the right people? Have they been targeted effectively?

Utilitarian motive—Is the emphasis on the core benefits of the offer, not flashy consumerist appeal?

Abstraction of the product—Can we see what you're selling? And if we can, would seeing it make us want to buy it? If the answer is no, B2B best practices indicate a creative approach that's less about the product and more about what it does and the benefits it delivers.

Masterclass needs to reach photographers, not just anybody. More specifically, they're looking for the kind of "prosumer" level photographers who take their hobby seriously and are committed to learning and improving.

If an investing robo-advisor platform runs their campaign like an e-commerce campaign, they will end up with a million people who aren't qualified, aren't depositing money, and ultimately don't contribute to returns on ad spend. They don't want just anybody to deposit money, they want people with hundreds of thousands of dollars to deposit.

Targeting by Vertical

SaaS (Software as a Service) is a big category and a big part of our business at Right Percent. Generally, the first "S" refers to digital tools for businesses to use. An HR SaaS would help Human Resource teams manage the hiring process and give performance reviews.

In many cases, companies will focus on specific verticals for their SaaS. So not every HR tool is for everyone, but HR tools for the medical profession, or something like that. This strategy has a trade-off—you have a smaller target market but, ideally, a higher conversion rate with each individual decision-maker. This intensifies everything and makes a leading indicator even more important because a smaller audience means fewer conversions. To reach your specific customer, you need even more precise targeting and messaging. Otherwise, you'll generate a large percentage of unqualified leads.

It often works well, though. We have many clients at Right Percent targeting very specific verticals, like childcare, dentists, construction, and cryptocurrency. We also almost always recommend that clients with large LinkedIn ad spends split their campaigns by vertical for optimal performance.

From a creative standpoint, niching-down means you need precise creative that really calls out your target audience directly.

For Childcare Directors

See why you'll never go back to pen and paper!

- Enrollment
- Tuition
- Check-in
- Daily sheets

brightwheel

It's also key to have differentiated ad creative. This also makes your ads look more effective.

As mentioned, the go-to strategy for mid-market and enterprise ads on LinkedIn is to have clients split their targeting into verticals. The reason this works on LinkedIn is because LinkedIn audiences work better when they're tighter as opposed to Facebook and Google, which are algorithmic and want more data. But the other reason to do this is we find they drive an increase in conversion events.

Channel and conversion event

Your channel of choice is going to follow the guidelines we've already covered: Facebook for B2SMB, LinkedIn for enterprise, Google if you have intent, other ad channels if you've mastered one of the big three channels and want to expand.

One thing about B2SMB verticals is that they can work with a surprisingly niche audience. For Brightwheel, we target childcare centers. For Boulevard, we go after hair salons. There are not that many of these places, so these are very verticalized campaigns that just go right to the target and call them out with great effect. So, with the right niche, the vertical approach works well, and you don't have to worry too much about audience size.

Niche audience/ Niche offer

It goes without saying that your offer should be catered to your target decision-maker. Obviously, a niche offer should be targeted to somebody in that niche. The same goes for incentives. If you're targeting childcare centers, don't get them an Amazon gift card as an incentive, try Michael's for arts and crafts supplies. Think about what the industry in your vertical values and incentivize accordingly.

Learning From Other Marketing Channels

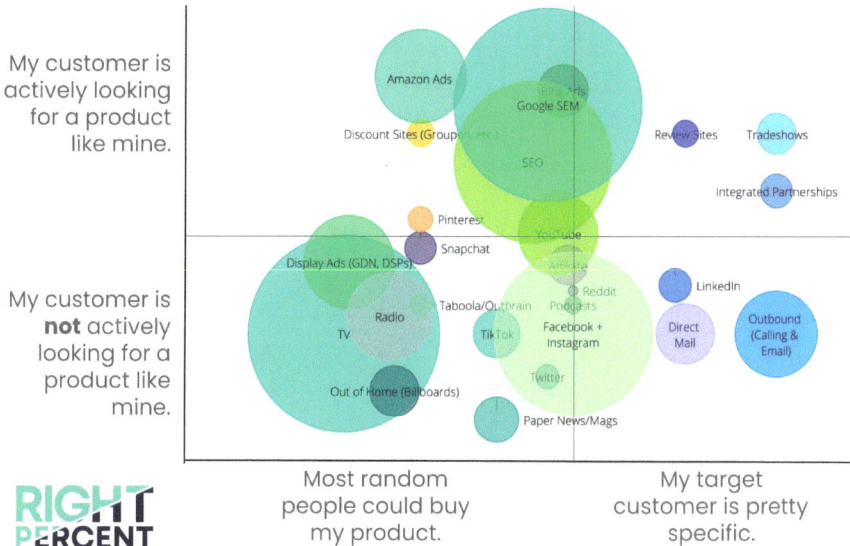

My customer is actively looking for a product like mine.

My customer is **not** actively looking for a product like mine.

Amazon Ads
Google SEM
Discount Sites (Groupon, etc.)
SEO
Review Sites
Tradeshows
Integrated Partnerships
Pinterest
Snapchat
YouTube
Display Ads (GDN, DSPs)
Affiliate
Reddit
LinkedIn
Taboola/Outbrain
Podcasts
Radio
TikTok
Facebook + Instagram
Direct Mail
Outbound (Calling & Email)
TV
Twitter
Out of Home (Billboards)
Paper News/Mags

Most random people could buy my product.

My target customer is pretty specific.

RIGHT PERCENT

As mentioned above, Facebook, Google and LinkedIn are the best advertising channels for B2B.

However, learnings from the other channels can greatly form and improve your ad strategy.

Here are some call-outs on those channels:

Outbound Sales

Many SaaS brands only have a sales team and do no ads whatsoever. They approach ads having built their business on the back of their sales team. This is especially true with companies targeting enterprise businesses. For companies already having success with cold selling, Facebook and LinkedIn ads are a natural fit. Paid social generally generates leads with lower intent than a warm inbound lead, but salespeople with experience in doing outbound have no problem selling to lower intent leads.

Referrals

Many early-stage, series-A or seed-stage companies have only acquired their customers through referrals. When a potential client has heard of them, they're warm leads. The prospect has usually done their research. These teams are used to leads who have convinced themselves they already want to buy and just need some handholding. These teams face a learning curve with ads because they're not used to difficult leads.

Trade shows and in-person events

These selling opportunities come with similar challenges to cold calling, but with a face-to-face twist. Trade shows are one of the best channels for reaching niche decision makers, since often conferences are one of the only places to find your target market in one place.

Business Development Partnerships

This means partnering with another company to share deal flows or pay for referrals. These can be life-changing deals when they work, but they're hard to do well. You face a chicken-and-egg problem where people only want to integrate with you if you're already big, but you need those integrations to become big. Having another growth channel can help you escape this dilemma.

Lever 2—Offer: Give Your Audience What They Want

It's in the name

Spelling bee rules tell us you're not supposed to use the word in defining the word, but offer is basically anything you're *offering* the client. It's the expectation you set in your ad. And it's probably the most underused of all the levers in B2B advertising because people don't think of it as a lever.

What's your offer?

Offer is another area where businesses consistently miss the mark without even knowing it. The bottom line is offering a demo is not sufficient in the current marketing environment. Every company I've seen scale past $100,000 in monthly spend on paid social with good ROI does so through effective use of content offers or incentive offers. There are no exceptions that I've seen. To get the offer right, you have to stop thinking of the offer as an afterthought and instead make your offer the basis of your campaign. A **content offer** would be an eBook, guide, tool, or checklist. Useful stuff, in other words. An **incentive offer** is a discount or promotion. There's a lot more to offers and how to find the right one for your campaign, and we'll get into that in the chapter on offers. From a myth-busting point of view, the thing to remember is that an offer is foundational to your campaign, not something you tack on after the fact.

What offer do we have that is most effective at promoting this goal to our defined audience?

Is it getting people to try a demo, or offering an incentive to meet with our team? Is it creating downloadable content behind a gated wall that we can use for further outreach and nurturing?

Offer types

There are three main offer types, broadly speaking.

Traditional

This is a demo, a 30-day free trial, or something similar. It's a straightforward "try before you buy" situation.

Content

This is probably the biggest and most effective category. It's offering people something useful to help them run their business. For B2Enterprise offers, this is usually knowledge in the form of an eBook, white paper, or report. Credibility and social proof matter with this audience.

For B2SMB, content offers tend to be checklists, templates, printouts, and other useful digital products. This audience doesn't care if you got your insights from Deloitte if you can help them solve a problem.

Much of the time, your target decision-makers are not ready to book a phone call with your sales team or try out your online demo. But people are always ready to download something useful to them.

A well-run content advertising campaign achieves three things for you:

1. You collect potential client contact information.
2. The reader associates your brand with useful tools.
3. Your sales team has a convenient launching point to upsell into your product

An effective content campaign is hyper-targeted to your most qualified audience. It should make them think, *"This is just for me."* It's important to directly relate your content to your value proposition. Checklists and templates do well because they are action-oriented, and your audience can see their value immediately. This is what LinkedIn calls "snackable" content, and it works.

Incentive

In this case, you're giving something in exchange for what you're asking. This could be a gift card or discount, something to sweeten the deal for your customer. As we mentioned before, it helps to add a personal touch here, like a Home Depot gift card for contractors instead of a boring Amazon gift card.

Nailing your offer

A well-run content campaign helps you get important client information, and it associates your brand with useful tools in the minds of your audience.

But it has to be good. You can't just put out garbage content to get email addresses and expect the sales team to take it from there. Your content should be a launching point for a natural upsell into your product.

The antidote to ad fatigue

One really cool and surprising thing we learned from our data on ads is that a great offer causes less ad fatigue over time. If all you're doing is offering a demo, you can expect to see your CTR drop off as people grow weary of seeing your ad.

RIGHT
PERCENT

Gated content **prevents ad fatigue** in B2B ad accounts.

Below is aggregated data. Ad accounts that only use "get a demo" ads and no content ads face headwinds from audience fatigue.

Click Through Rate of Ad Accounts over Time

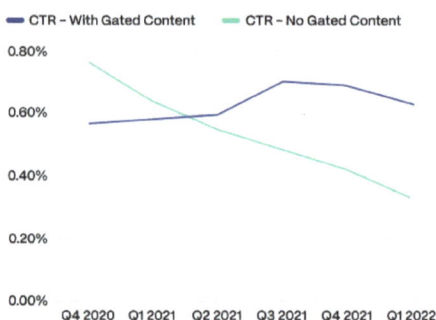

— CTR – With Gated Content   — CTR – No Gated Content

0.80%

0.60%

0.40%

0.20%

0.00%

Q4 2020 Q1 2021 Q2 2021 Q3 2021 Q4 2021 Q1 2022

Offering a variety of gated content keeps your numbers up. The reason is simple. People get sick of you imploring them to "try our product." Your audience just tunes out mentally after a while. It's human nature. But if there's a new eBook every 45 days, they don't tune it out, they actually do the opposite. This is a vital best practice for long-term success in ads.

Ad fatigue is the bane of all mature ad accounts. If an account has been running for years and has high spend, and it's just consistently getting worse even though there's nothing else happening in the market causing the drop, the answer is usually ad fatigue. This is like the universal law of entropy. Ad fatigue takes over eventually.

Offer is one of your tools to delay ad fatigue. The other is creative, which we'll cover in that section. The other tool you have is changing your audience, because a new audience, by definition, hasn't had time to get sick of your ads. But eventually, they too will hit the point of fatigue.

Note: Audience fatigue is a paid social or attention-based marketing issue where you have a fixed audience whose attention you're trying to capture. In search, the issue is not fatigue but impression share. Both are an issue of getting all the juice you can squeeze out of your campaign. But because ad fatigue isn't an issue in search, you can generally run search campaigns for longer.

How's your Funnel?

Your offer and your funnel are intrinsically linked.

Generally speaking, your sales funnel starts with a click. Someone's interested in your ad and attracted to your offer. After clicking your ad, they then go to some kind of experience, either it's your website, a native lead form, or something to download. The important thing from a funnel perspective is to know what the user's expectations are when they get to the website and what you want them to do.

If you collect information, do everything you can to qualify that lead. Qualifying questions could include:

How many employees do you have?
Have you used a product like ours before?
What is your budget?

The answers to these questions are correlated to revenue for potential clients.

For early-stage companies, the goal is to find out what works. Where can you find product-channel fit? Where should you focus your limited time and effort? For that reason, you should err on the side of asking more qualifying questions, not less.

Even though it may decrease your conversion rate, you must learn which qualifying answers correlate to future revenue. Knowing the indicators you can rely on is what unlocks your future performance.

You can go deeper with questions that give you qualification and intent. Questions like:

How soon are you ready to purchase?

Do you want to schedule a demo?

Armed with qualifying information, there are a lot of ways you can route that info to your sales team. For best results, you'll want to set aside a group of salespeople with leads from ads, or just one salesperson if you're small. The reason for this is warmth. If you have a sales team that's dealing with warm leads, as is often the case in a business doing something that works, when you bring them a few ad leads, they will fail because your salespeople won't spend time chasing down those ad leads. It's easier to just close the warm leads.

On the other hand, if you've got a team of hunters who are skilled at closing cold leads, ads will help you scale their activities, and they'll probably love having all these social leads to call on. The important thing, in this dynamic, is to call leads quickly as part of your funnel. There's good data that indicates the exponential decay in pickup rate if you delay your call. That rate is something like 10 times higher if you call within the first 10 minutes vs. the first hour. You must make the most of this recency when you make your approach. The hard truth is your form isn't nearly as important to them as it is to you. So, make the call. Don't delay.

The PLG funnel

In the product-led growth (PLG) paradigm, there are no salesperson touches, but generally you want to get leading indicators the same way, based on how people track.

So, for instance, for almost all PLG companies, there's some action customers can take, whether that's creating their first Trello board, uploading their first property, etc. The same power law of recency applies. If they don't do it within the first 24 hours, they will never do it. Action is your leading indicator.

Are we living in or heading to a post-funnel world?

There's another type of funnel in advertising which does not work, and this is the one people are talking about when they say, "the funnel is dead" or "we're living in a post-funnel world."

The "dead" funnel is the old marketing AIDA loop, which stands for "Awareness Interest Desire Action." There are a bunch of versions of this. People who think they understand social might swap one of the "A"s for "Attention."

In theory, it's supposed to work like this:

You have a giant *awareness* audience that targets people on Facebook. Let's say it's people who watched a video. They then retarget viewers of the video and serve them ads.

This structure has its origin in the old days of digital advertising when algorithmic targeting was no good. You couldn't trust the platform to just find your customers for you, so you would build your own audience by making educated guesses based on their viewing habits or what they said about themselves in their profile.

Nowadays, the algorithm is so much better, and the AIDA approach is wildly inefficient. That layered approach to ads just doesn't work anymore, and nobody should even think about doing it. You can always add retargeting to a campaign, but when it comes to social, you're better off working from the assumption that all users are in consideration at all times. Anyway, there's no real difference between awareness and consideration in practice when it comes to ads. You can assume that anybody might be willing to get your eBook. You can't know for sure, but the algorithm will steer you in the right direction.

There are some exceptions to this, however. For example, a CRM platform with good intent data, that has somehow figured out that a given company is interested in switching platforms, that kind of precise targeting could work, but that's expensive and a unique exception that proves the rule.

But when people say, "the funnel is dead," they don't mean the funnel as in the step-by-step process of closing a sale. They're talking about that tiered structure that really has no place in a modern social campaign.

"Nobody wants to give you their email" and other nonsense from LinkedIn influencers

Later, we'll have a whole section where I rant about bad LinkedIn advice, but I want to bust one persistent myth adjacent to the "dead funnel" right now.

The hot take is that the traditional B2B funnel is totally dead and that collecting MQLs is a pointless errand for B2B businesses. According to them, nobody wants to submit their email and nobody wants gated content.

All of that is what it is, and you could debate the wisdom of those points all day. But the real issue is the disastrous alternative to the dead funnel, which is to just do no tracking beyond putting the question, "where did you hear about us?" in your form. No iteration. No learning. No way to improve. No way to know which campaign is working vs. not.

This is a baby with the bathwater situation, where MQLs are written off totally over a few natural limitations. I prefer to look at lead gen with MQLs the way Churchill thought of democracy, "the worst system in the world . . . except for all the other ones."

The laboratory funnel vs. market reality

So much discussion around funnel best practices is based in a theoretical understanding of the funnel in a vacuum where it's marketing's job is to create the lead, and sale's job is to close it. These two roles exist in hermetic independence. But that's not how it works in the real world because the sales team has a huge impact on lead quality and the ability to close said lead.

The language you use in your ad creative, the strength of your offer, these are marketing decisions that strongly impact the likelihood of a close. These steps don't exist in a vacuum. At the end of the day, marketing is responsible for generating closable leads and generating revenue. Your marketing team can't just wash their hands of the final close, not when they have so many levers to influence it.

Troubleshooting your offer

If you're not doing well on paid social, it's almost always safe to assume that your offer could be better.

There are three golden rules of content offers:

1. It should be highly focused on your target decision-maker's pain points.

   That may sound obvious, but folks often underestimate just how focused it needs to be. Talk directly to the person you want so they say, "wow, this content is for me!"

2. Your content should be closely related to your unique value proposition.

   So, if you're Bill.com, who make account receivable and payroll software, you should not be promoting content about working from home because your sales team can't do anything with that. There's no qualification and no upselling opportunity. Whereas a checklist to make sure you don't miss anything when paying invoices would give your sales team a chance to point out that Bill does everything on that checklist automatically. In the case of demo ads, your offer should help the customer sell themselves on your product.

3. Your content should be actionable.

   Bad content is often too vague or abstract. It could be full of good information, but the reader can't immediately see how it's useful to them and how it can make their life better. This is why checklists and templates do so well (and why we've included some in this book).

One Right Percent client has had years of success on the back of an ad for a spreadsheet template for budgeting in their niche target market. Their audience loves it because it solves a real problem for them. Their sales team loves it because it tees up sales calls nicely. They can say, "Hey, I'm glad you're enjoying the template, but our software does the same thing only automated and better." The ad itself uses a screenshot of the spreadsheet. It's a simple ad, but it shows people an offer they can imagine using and clearly see the value of.

Zenefits
Sponsored

Does your company have an employee handbook going over your mission statement, products, and benefits?
We've made an easy to use tool to either build or improve any employee handbook.

Create an employee handbook in minutes.

Free Employee Handbook Tool
zenefits.com/handbook

Download

4.7K   435 Comments 13 Shares

Like   Comment

Lever 3—Conversion Event: Train Your Team and the Algorithm

Conversion events are how you and the ad platform learn what's working. Without conversion events, you're flying blind to how well your ad campaigns do. Most of what you do in B2B ads uses the conversion event as your north star of optimization.

What is a conversion event?

In a perfect world, you would spend a dollar for someone to give you ten. Advertising would just be a perpetual motion money-generating machine. Now, in practice, you may end up getting such a return—that's the amazing thing about ads. But you don't get that money the moment they click on your ad, so you need a conversion event to indicate the likelihood of a future payday on the back of your ad spend.

A conversion event is anything that the prospective customer does when interacting with your ad, product, or site, that's trackable and that you've chosen to label as important.

In e-commerce, the most important conversion events are adding an item to the cart and clicking the checkout button. Those are two distinct conversion events that could trigger unique email flows or ad targeting.

In B2B, the most common conversion event would be filling out a lead form. They could do that on your website or in a native lead ad. You can use a lead form to further qualify a conversion event. You might have a question on the form that asks how many employees they have and only count their response as a conversion event if they have 200+ employees, or whatever number you're looking for.

Big leads

There are so many possibilities for conversion events. You could make a rule that says if someone gets to page three on a multipage form, that's a qualified conversion. You could go offline and say that someone only becomes a conversion if your sales team switches them from a lead to an opportunity. The PLG version might be qualifying them when they upload their credit card info.

The important thing is that you, as the business owner, choose what the conversion event is.

What's the value of a lead?

A lot happens between the initial click and actually making money—funnels, sales calls, and multiple processes that engage different teams and cost centers across your company. It can be difficult to determine exactly what a lead is worth and the true cost of nurturing that lead into a customer.

This is why it's so important to keep testing and keep learning. You might look at your data to find that half of sales come from companies with 50-100 employees. If that's the case, you might define your conversion event as a lead coming from a company of that size and use that as the measuring stick for your campaigns. Over time, you'll evolve and dial in the exact mix of variables of action they've taken on the site, along with feedback from customers, to get the right conversion event.

Marketers need to Create L.I.F.E

To address the problem of the unknowns and data gaps that are hurting your business, you need to Create LIFE:

Leading
Indicators of
Future
Earnings

The key to unlocking so much of the potential of B2B advertising is finding a way to understand the value of leads and clicks *before* they convert. When a lead visits your website or comes in from a campaign, what did they do on your site that indicates a likelihood that person is going to convert into a customer in the future? And what do you know about the size of that customer? This is something few B2B companies do well . . . or at all.

Creating LIFE is critical because it saves time. Generally, B2B sales take a while to close B2SMB can take a month, B2Enterprise could take a year. Without the insights provided by LIFE, you have to wait for every campaign to play out and then do a post-mortem on your sales and attribution. On the other hand, when you start with the right variables and look for those leading indicators, you can estimate the value of those leads in advance. This gives you so much more control. You have the power to edit and optimize your campaigns for the results you want rather than having to reset and try again for different results considering how a long and disappointing campaign played out.

Rules for conversion events

You want at least 30-50 conversion events per week per campaign or ad-set.

That means if your conversion event is someone filling out a lead form, you want at least 30 of these per week. The reason for this is that the platforms don't do well with limited amounts of data. They're not good at learning. So, you want as many conversions as possible within each ad set. If that number starts going over 50, it's time to focus on quality over volume (which we'll get to in a second).

You want conversions to be as far down the funnel as possible

You want conversions to correlate with revenue. Someone who gets to page three out of five on your form is more qualified than someone who just fills out page one.

High quality leads lead to revenue

Pop quiz:

Campaign A has 50 regular leads and 40 high-quality leads.
Campaign B has 100 regular leads and 20 high-quality leads.
Which one is going to lead to more revenue?
Answer: the one with more high-quality leads

Conversion events fuel iteration

Lead quality drives two key forces in B2B ads: iteration and cyclicality. Each conversion event is a learning opportunity—you gain insights, the platform adapts, you make adjustments, and as more conversions follow, the cycle of improvement continues. That's the basis of marketing today.

The balance is finding the right depth and quality of conversion event vs. volume of conversions.

If you're only getting 10 new customers per month, how many conversion events are you really going to have? When you're small, you're going to prioritize volume. But as you get bigger and deal with more volume, you can start prioritizing quality. A company handling thousands of B2B conversions per month can maximize value by focusing on the highest-quality leads with the strongest signals. Bigger companies also have a leg up on some tech integrations that help with collecting and interpreting data. They just have more data to work with, generally. For smaller companies, the advantage, even though they have less data, is that they're scrappier and can talk to their leads directly and be closer to the qualitative side of things. With all this talk of data and iteration, never underestimate the value of a real conversation.

Channel considerations

Leading indicators tend to work the same way on different channels. What works on Facebook will work on search. However, there are a few differences worth mentioning. One is that Facebook and LinkedIn have excellent native lead capabilities, where the user can create the lead directly on the platform and send it to your CRM.

Example Native Lead Form:

Google has a terrible native lead option that doesn't work for anybody. You can have native conversion events on LinkedIn and Facebook, but not Google.

What if I'm not getting the leading indicators I want?

What do you do if you're not getting those higher-quality leads you're after? Let's say you're asking if they have 50+ employees, but you're only getting leads with fewer than 20. It's time to go back to your levers.

Is your creative targeting the right people?

Is your audience correct to reach the kind of people you want?

If it's too small, maybe you should be on LinkedIn and not Facebook, in which case it's time to take another look at channel and strategy.

Pick up the phone for intent

There are a couple of optional form fields that I have found to be very useful. One is for content ads. Now, a side note: many companies are hesitant about content ads because they don't want to be a turn-and-burn sales operation that constantly calls people. But they can work well if executed properly.

What you can do is ask people if they'd like a demo call. I find that 30-40% say yes for most B2B companies. So, you have half as many leads coming from these campaigns, but they're higher intent to close into customers. Once you're on a demo call, there are some really good high-intent qualification questions you can ask:

How soon do you want to buy this product?

Have you bought similar products before?

Or you can just ask about their intent: *How serious are you?*

Sales teams love these questions because they provide better insights and serve as a strong indicator whether these leads are likely to convert or not. So, be straightforward with your qualifying questions.

How Advertising Differs for Sales-led vs Product-led Companies

We've covered the general pros and cons of the main channels, now let's talk about finding the right channel for what you're serving up to your audience. There's a lot to this, but it has to do the customer experience and what you want to happen next.

Are they going to go to your sales team?

Are they going to sign up for a demo through your website?

Sales-Led Growth is the more traditional B2B growth strategy.

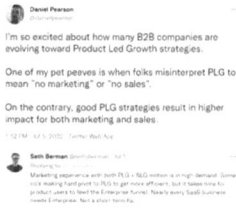

Discussion of PLG vs SLG on Twitter

In SLG, the name of the digital advertising game is Marketing Qualified Leads (MQLs), and the way you play best is through gated content.

The core of your job as an SLG advertiser is to get the customer to raise their hand. It's sales' job to take this warm, real person who is raising their hand and make them convert. People are surprisingly amenable to upsells from content if the content is right.

The two keys to content ad success are to make content that is:

Laser-focused on your target audience

Closely related to your value proposition

For clients, we often see content with the above characteristics close at 60% the rate of "get a demo" MQLs, but at 30% of the cost per MQL.

Once you have good content, you have to focus on your optimization event. In SLG, any bad leads that slip to the sales team have a real price to the business because they waste sales time and lower morale.

PLG means your company doesn't have a big sales team, which means raw MQLs or "leads" (people who fill out a lead form and nothing else) are not very useful to you. Instead, you want people to use your product.

It would be great if the people using your product were from big, rich companies. But it doesn't make that much of a difference if people who can't afford your product use it since your marginal cost per user is very low, and they might convert to big users one day.

So, your conversion events to prioritize are more about usage than qualification. You need to create and optimize on an event that you think will correlate to revenue at some time.

There are two contenders for this conversion event for PLG companies:

Account Created: This is pretty straightforward: if a new user creates an account, you can optimize on it.

Remember, you need at least 30 conversions per week per ad-set to let the ad platform algorithms learn. If you don't get 30 new accounts per week, you have to optimize on something higher in the funnel, like step 2 out of 6 in the sign-up flow or something like that.

One major risk even with 'Account Created' is that many people create an account but never actually use the product. You really don't want to trick yourself into thinking you're driving engaged users when you're not. Often, if customers don't at least test the product within 24 hours they never will. Which leads us to contender #2.

Product Usage: This means you optimize when the user actually does something in the free trial. "First Trello Board Created" or "First Invoice Uploaded" or "First Team Member Added." This is usually a really powerful signal and one we recommend often.

One way to try to sign up bigger companies is to add another variable before counting the signal—like "First Team Member Added + Company Size > 50 Employees." The risk is that you can get too few signals to optimize on. The gain is that if you get enough signals, the algorithms will start sending you bigger and more valuable leads.

Often, developer teams balk at adding pixel tracking to the product. Ideally, you can convince them. If not, you'll have to rely on only server-to-server integrations to send conversion events directly to the platforms.

Getting this right is 100% necessary to your success. It lets you iterate correctly on campaigns.

Google, LinkedIn and Facebook work for both. For paid social, creative is very important and you should follow B2B best practices.

For SLG, use effective content to find hand-raisers for your sales team, optimize on big leads and pre-qualify with creative.

For PLG, optimize on a conversion event that demonstrates product usage and correlates to revenue eventually.

Lever 4—Creative: Talk to Your Audience the Right Way

If advertising were a restaurant . . .

"If advertising were a restaurant, Creative is the front of the house. It's the wait-staff and the maître d' for your product. It has to look presentable and be fast on its feet, serving up what's cooking. It's their job to know the menu inside and out, make specials sound appetizing, and convey the chef's passion to people who aren't really listening half the time."

—Colin Maguire, Director of Content Strategy at Right Percent

We're not hawking toasters

One of the biggest differences between B2B and B2C creative is that with B2B, the product is almost always abstract. The problem with selling an API or a dashboard or some kind of system is that it's very hard to show in a single image or short video exactly how the product works. Visuals just don't represent it well. With B2C, on the other hand, you're almost always selling a concrete product, be it boxer briefs, or a toaster. That's why user-generated content (UGC) has worked so well for B2C brands on social media, because you can just show someone using a toaster, maybe in a way that makes it clear why your toaster is better.

This abstractness in B2B is why text-heavy ads work so well. The ones we see working best use that text to call out the target decision-maker, in effect saying,

"Hey, you, stop what you're doing and look at this."

"Hey, childcare director . . ."

"Hey, marketing manager . . ."

Follow that up with a compelling offer when you get their attention, all the while keeping the focus on its relevance to them in particular. You can crush it with ads that are 80% text. And this goes against every piece of conventional wisdom out there on how to do ads. Most people think they need a visual anchor, an iconic logo, or a cartoon mascot for their ads, but that's simply not true with B2B. That's not to say you can't have creative imagery, but the text has to be straightforward.

*You have to get the attention of the business decision-maker **in a second**, as they're browsing their feed or the web.*

You're not as clever as you think you are

The problem is that advertising professionals love to be clever. It makes sense, clever ads are the stuff of advertising books and awards. But they're the worst kind of ads performance-wise. They always underperform because people are just scrolling when they encounter your ad, and they don't really care. They're not going to stop mid-scroll and appreciate your cleverness. The exception to this is with imagery: you can be as clever as you want there. But your text and headline have to be testing positioning statements. No exceptions.

Be as funny as you want with your images. But your text has to be credible and concrete.

The same goes for videos, your positioning statement needs to show up in the subtitles in the first three seconds, or you're toast.

Seriously, nobody cares

This point bears repeating because it's so counter to what most people think makes a good ad. Cleverness doesn't work because it takes time (even just a second) to appreciate your cleverness, and nobody has as much as a second to spend figuring out your wit. They truly don't care about your company, and they don't care about your ad that's flashing in front of them between reels and memes in their infinite scroll.

Visual headlines for the win

I've tested at least 10,000 B2B ads over the last 10 years, and the results are clear: **Your visual headline accounts for 75% of the performance of the ad**. So, getting that text right is more important than everything else combined. The visual headline needs to be your main focus and the main thing you test.

This is yet another case of simply doing what works. These ads don't look like what your typical advertiser has in mind. It's not going to win you awards, but it's what we see working consistently with every client. When we run our own ads against others, it's the one with big text in the ad as a headline or broken up as a checklist that always wins. Always.

Where to find your visual headlines

Visual headlines are everywhere. They're your product features, the benefits, the audience you're calling out. If you're stumped for a visual headline, try talking to your product team or your sales folks. It's good to get both of those perspectives because they can vary so much and give different positioning statements to test. The product manager will look at product data and how people use the product, while the salesperson will know what customers find important and what they're actually thinking about your product.

Be specific

Cleverness's fashionable cousin is artsy-ness. Artsy ads don't work because they're broad and vague. We know that specificity is what works best.

This can be a real struggle with big companies who like the sound of their own name a little too much and lose sight of what the customer is looking for.

If I'm a fleet manager, I'm going to stop scrolling when I see an ad calling out fleet managers. If I'm a developer, seeing something in the format of *Hacker News* is going to grab me. You have milliseconds to grab your audience, so be specific.

But isn't there a rule about text in ads?

Not anymore. It used to be that Facebook had a rule stating that only 20% of your ad could have text on it. But that rule no longer exists, and the best ads on Facebook tend to be text-heavy.

The T-shirt loophole

One workaround that originates in the days of that Facebook rule is to put your text on an object in the ad. We don't do as many of these as we used to because of brand standards, but we have found that putting text on a t-shirt can work insanely well. Some of our best ads have been designed that way.

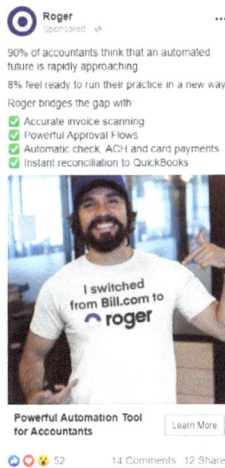

We recommend putting headlines on white space — but you can often superimpose text effectively on shirts and books.

Why 9?

There's a good reason why we test nine visual headlines at once. Ad performance follows a power law, where a small percentage of ads generate the majority of the impact. Of the 20 fresh ads you put on Facebook, one of them is going to get around 90% of your spend. Of all the headlines and positioning statements we test, almost none of them are going to be seen by anyone, so getting them perfect in the name of aesthetics is just silly and a total waste of time. Quibbling over an Oxford comma gets you nowhere. You just can't be married to your copy. You have to let data drive what's working. As long as something is on-brand and isn't offensive, misleading, or illegal, just run it because you won't know anything until you do.

You don't need to be a perfectionist

The power law is why it's very important not to spend forever going back and forth over the text of any given ad. If you strive for perfection and do a full court press on every line of copy, there's too much friction. You won't get enough tested, and you won't have enough positioning statements to find out what works. Irony of ironies, trying to do it perfectly will keep you from being able to find out what's good and what's not.

We tend to come back to clients with about 20 ads. They'll cut about three or so, and we'll run the others. Friction is the death of creative in advertising, so get comfortable just putting out tons of positioning statements as fast as you can.

Focus on what matters

Nail the visual headline, come up with a bunch of positioning statements to test aggressively. Be a comedian or a poet in your free time.

Testing copy is like playing Battleship

Colin, our head of strategy, compares ads to a game of Battleship. You just throw as much as you can out there and see what's getting hits.

The copywriter has to come up with words that can be tested. He or she is more of a salesperson than an artist. This point has to be hammered home for everyone on the creative side of ads. No matter how much you hem and haw over a headline, you just don't know until you test. Realistically, one in 20 is going to get all the ad spend while the others are seen by virtually no one, so getting them perfect in the name of aesthetics is just silly and a total waste of time.

As Colin points out,

"I have had so many ads I thought were bangers. I was convinced they were so good, and they just never got any spend while one or two that I wrote in a hurry to fill out the brief got like 60% of the lift."

Creative drives lead quality

Another big misconception I want to smash here is that the creative doesn't impact lead quality. This goes back to the problem of marketing teams thinking it's their job to find leads and it's sales' job to close them. But the truth is marketing has so many levers to affect lead quality. For instance, you can add pricing to your ads to dissuade companies that aren't a good fit for your product from clicking.

Qualification through your competitors

Another way to qualify your leads is by adding brand names of competitors or complements with a similar price point. So, if you're competing with Salesforce, anyone who can afford them can afford you.

Same with integrations. If you call out that you integrate with Salesforce, you can qualify Salesforce users and folks who can afford that kind of solution. If you're trying to attract high-value users, put the emphasis on the features high-value users care about. If you're looking for enterprise clients, call out the features that differentiate your enterprise plan.

This goes back to T-shirt machines and is one of the main things that differentiates B2B and B2C. Whereas everyone can buy a B2C product, B2B depends on qualification because not everyone can buy them.

Don't talk about yourself

This is one of the golden rules of advertising, but in B2B the tendency towards narcissism takes on a very particular twist. B2B companies have a bad habit of talking about their internal operations. Acme Business Corp will talk about the fact that this new product line is managed by such and such a division and what that means to them and to their customers. But there's a huge disconnect in that kind of messaging because, in reality, all that internal gossip doesn't matter AT ALL outside the company. **Keep your focus on what matters to the customer.**

Keep the offer in the headline

The headline cannot exist independently from the offer. The visual headline and the offer are intertwined. You only come up with your headline once you have an offer to start with. Again, this is why offers always come first and dictate everything you do. Your visual headline is your scroll-stopper.

Don't underestimate a mook with a framework

In the 2010 book MADE TO STICK, there's a study where scientists ran a controlled experiment to test the power of a success framework based on leading with the offer. In it they had three control groups: ad professionals, mooks off the street, and mooks who used the framework. After running the ads that the three teams came up with, the winners were the untrained mooks who used the framework. They beat the mooks who didn't have the framework. But, surprisingly, they also beat the advertising professionals.

Clever doesn't work, but unexpected can

Emotion works. Concrete examples work. And going in an unexpected direction works. Two classic B2C examples of this are Domino's Pizza LOOK UP campaign, promoting their new recipe by acknowledging that their old one was no good, and Patagonia telling people not to buy their jackets. This can be wildly effective in B2B too. The difference between unexpected and clever is that a clever ad is basically telling everyone, "see what I did there?" It's a pathetic bid for attention. Whereas something unexpected actually deserves their attention and often stops them mid-scroll.

You are interrupting

Creative cuts through the fog of people's scrolling and search experience. If you're using LinkedIn, for example, you need to understand that you are interrupting people, whether they're networking in earnest, or just doom-scrolling at work. Your aim should be to use creative to instantly communicate your value and speak directly to stakeholders. So, if you're trying to reach HR managers, you need to make it clear in the millisecond you have to stop their scroll, that you're talking directly to HR managers. You do this with a strong visual headline and words to back it up baked into an image.

There's a time and a place for jargon

Generally speaking, jargon is the enemy of good copywriting and good writing in general. It's something I've been trying to avoid in this book, except when it's necessary for technical reasons. After all, advertising is jargon-heavy, and words like "creative" have a unique and exact meaning in this game.

That said, jargon can be a powerful asset when trying to drive down CPC.

When you're paying per click, unqualified clicks cost you. Jargon can help you by acting as a qualifier. By using industry and vertical jargon in your visual headline, you can instantly rule out laypeople who you're not trying to reach in the first place. This works for the same reason avoiding jargon is a best practice in other forms of writing: Because it makes your writing inaccessible. But you want your ads to be inaccessible to people who would be wasting your money and their time by clicking on them.

Just remember, there's an art to using jargon, and a little bit can go a long way. Don't just throw a bunch of big techie buzzwords at the wall and see what sticks. Instead, try to use jargon in the same way you would call out specific decision-maker roles.

When we worked with Boulevard, a company that makes booking software for hair salons, we were getting a lot of clicks from hairdressers who were just renting a chair in a salon and weren't in a position to make stakeholder decisions for the salon. To counter this, we decided to get a little more jargon-y and use words only salon owners would relate to. It made a big difference, and that change alone drove down their CPC significantly.

You need a system to review ads

The more friction in the process, the less creative you'll test, and the worse your account will perform over time because you're not testing enough ad creative.

Ideally you have one person on the client side who approves copy, but make sure that person knows the objective is not to be a perfectionist about every line, but to test as many positioning statements as possible.

There are three big barriers to getting creative tested

1. The brand team

Most companies have someone in charge of making sure everything produced is on brand. This is a very important job, but whoever's in this role has to consider how modern ad platforms work. One way they hinder team success is by enforcing overly rigid language and design rules in an effort to maintain brand standards.

This is another place where doing what works can run counter to conventional branding wisdom. While there's a time and a place for brand standards and a clear identity, adhering to them too rigidly can hurt your ads. For example, needing to use the same colors in every ad can condition an audience to start ignoring that ad. A little flexibility is key. Work with your brand people to find your limits so you can experiment while maintaining brand standards.

2. Legal

Companies, especially in highly regulated industries, have to be careful with what they claim and what they write. Legal review is a must, but it's also a source of delays and back-seat editing that can bog you down creatively for weeks and doom your campaign.

The best way by far to remedy this is to work upfront with your legal team and get a comprehensive checklist of things you're allowed to say and what you'll need to take to them for legal approval. With a long list of pre-approved claims, you can mix and match that language, knowing you're all good as far as legal is concerned. When you have a new product or are taking a new approach in your messaging, you can work with legal to review everything ahead of time and give you language you can work with.

3. Taste

This one's a little more abstract and it can be maddening if you don't find a concrete and methodical approach to accounting for subjective taste. Generally, you have to get your ads past the decision maker who's approving them and the CMO. This is why aligning everyone on best practices for ads is so crucial. You have to make it clear that only 5-10% of the ads you bring them are going to be successful and that it's in everybody's best interests to play around and be flexible in testing what works and what doesn't. Assuming what you're doing is on-brand and legal (see friction points 1 & 2) then just try some things and let them decide what they like based on what works.

Check your in-house ego

If you're working with an agency or outside creative talent, there's no need for your in-house talent to be afraid. The emphasis should always be on doing what works and what performs. Outside talent is there to help, not to stage a hostile takeover. Nobody should care if the winning ad comes from the in-house team or outside creative.

Create LIFE with campaign consolidation

Very few ads are going to lead to closed deals that report revenue, so, once again, you are going to rely on leading indicators.

From a creative standpoint, this is why campaign consolidation is an effective part of ad testing. If you have five different campaigns, each spending $10,000 a month and each one has its own ads, your conversion events and data will be spread pretty thin. Whereas if you roll all of those into one campaign, each ad will get five times as much spend. You'll get so much more data on those ads, allowing the platform for the conversion to do its magic, and you'll be getting more people in the door, so your team will be able to tell whether the ad is generating more qualified users.

This is everything because if you don't have a good conversion event and you're testing ads, you could have an ad that generates a lot of leads, but those leads don't convert and you'll be missing out and not knowing why.

What else works?

We've gone over visual headlines, big text, checklists, and text-heavy ads. Here are some other things that can work.

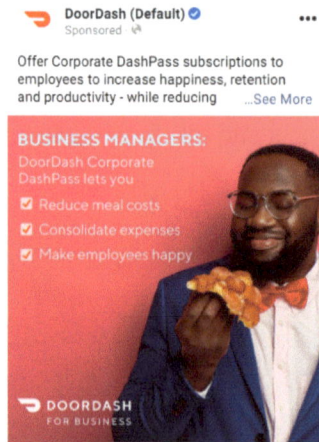

Checklist ads are a top performer on most of our accounts.

As I mentioned earlier, clever copy doesn't work, but clever visuals can. This could be something funny, ironic, or even metaphorical.

Credible & concrete

Testimonials can be very effective. It's important to know the difference between a testimonial that works and one that will do nothing for you. The best testimonials are credible, concrete, and/or have an emotional story. This one by DoorDash was a winner.

UI ads

SaaS UI ads can work, but they're tricky. Brand teams hate to hear this, but they usually do better when following the basic rules of big text before and after the UI image, which tends to look really tacky but often works.

Something to consider is client-related imagery. Anything that makes someone know at a glance, *this is for me.* One way you can do this is by making the ad imagery related to what you're selling. It may sound obvious, but if you're advertising something to do with painting, have painting stuff in the ad.

Eye lines and arrows

People follow arrows in images. People follow the eye lines of people in images. So, an ad where the person in the image is looking at the text you want the viewer to read will do better.

Forget explainer videos

The typical animated "explainer video" doesn't really work as an ad. They require the audience to have the patience to sit through. They're also expensive and time-consuming to produce.

The exception would be short walkthroughs that demonstrate how a product works, explaining the UI along the way. Those can be effective.

Videos have a "three-second rule" if you can get their attention in the first three seconds, you've got them for the next 15 to 30, but you've got to capture them in those first three seconds.

Ads that don't look like ads

We've had a few ads outperform everything because they don't look like ads. That's another general principle to keep in mind: Ads do better when they don't immediately get shut off as ads in people's minds. This is why big text works where neat formatting and on-brand color schemes fail, because people see the formatting, realize it's an ad, and ignore it.

On writing well

Writing ads solely based on how you've seen them done before and relying on your swipe file may seem like sound advice, but it can lead to trouble when crafting the kind of ads we're discussing. Writing B2B ads with traditional copywriting best practices in mind results in surface-level copy that doesn't communicate the value of your offer because it's too busy letting you know how clever the copywriter is. You want to stay away from what Colin calls "billboard statements," broad generalities that don't make it clear what you're offering, who you're speaking to, or what your offer will do for them.

The power of *why?*

You get away from superficial copy by asking *why?* Until you find the deeper, more substantial value you're trying to communicate your ads aren't going to convert. So, for example, let's say the benefit of your product "makes employees happy."

That's nice, but let's go deeper.

Why do you want to make your employees happier?

Less turnover, they'll stick around.

Why do you want less turnover?

It's expensive. It costs more to replace a seat, or worse, deal with a revolving door of unhappy quitters, than it is to keep an existing employee happy.

Now you have something you can call out in your copy that's much stronger and more specific than "happier employees." You could go with something like,

Reduce employee churn this quarter. Or *cut employee churn by 60%.*

These aren't amazing, but they're better than "happier employees." Words like "churn" and speaking in "quarters" subtly speak to an enterprise audience.

Know your audience

Identify your intended reader, then find ways to make them the hero of your writing. How can you make it clear to them that this product will help make them better at what they do, look good when it's time for their next promotion, or save the company money? Without understanding these motivating factors, you're leaving money on the table by failing to speak to what your audience really cares about.

This might involve some research. So, if you're talking about reducing churn, get ahold of some numbers. How much are you reducing churn by? What are the savings of that reduction? You can put those numbers in the copy or in a footnote indicated by an asterisk in the copy or headline.

Speaking of numbers, listing the price can be a great way to scare away unqualified clicks and make it clear that this is a B2B product.

Ad fatigue and the war for attention

If you're working with long sales cycles, ad fatigue isn't just a matter of running out of new people to reach. You also have to think about not wearing down current leads while they're still in the funnel. Try to keep your ads appealing and value-adds for anyone who sees them. Targeting's never going to be perfect, and some people at the bottom of the funnel are bound to encounter your top-of-funnel stuff. Just make sure it's not cringe.

Recap: The Levers of B2B Advertising

The levers of B2B ads are the main variables you can influence to affect a result from an ad account.

1. Audience—Who you're targeting and where you're reaching them.
2. Offer—What the user gets by clicking on your ad.
3. Conversion event—What you're measuring as the result of users clicking the ad.
4. Creative & copy—The words and visuals (or visual headlines) in your ad, tested for effectiveness.

Channel-Specific Guides

Most companies find major success with one channel that outstrips all the others. And that really should be the goal. There's a popular misconception that you are going to have 10 channels, each with 10% of your business, but that's generally not the way it works. Your aim is to find product-channel fit and scale as much as you can on the winning channels.

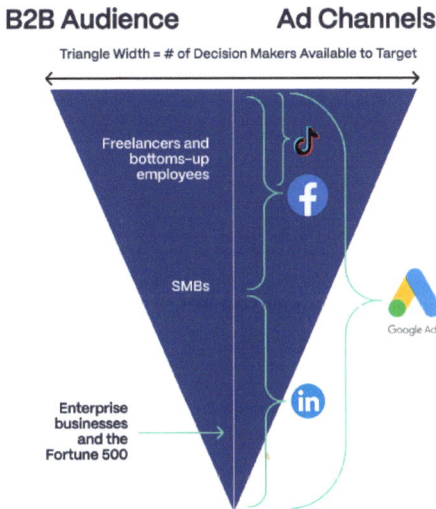

B2B audience size impacts
channel ad strategy

B2B Audience   **Ad Channels**

Triangle Width = # of Decision Makers Available to Target

Freelancers and
bottoms-up
employees

SMBs

Google Ads

Enterprise
businesses
and the
Fortune 500

Finding this sweet spot is intuitive when you follow the steps we've laid out so far and ask yourself the right questions. Like, how specific is your target audience?

More specific = LinkedIn

Less specific = Facebook.

Why Google and not Bing?

You'll notice that our channel-specific guide to paid search only talks about Google, and throughout this book, we use "Google" and "paid search" interchangeably. The reason for that is simple: Nobody uses Bing or Yahoo. Google has something like 90% market share, making them, for all intents and purposes, the only search engine worth talking about. They also have more sophisticated ad tools and targeting, but these are inexorably tied to their size and market share. A Bing campaign could only add an extra 10% marginal scale to your campaigns. Basically, you can just take your winning Google campaigns and apply them to Bing, so we don't need a separate Bing section.

Channel myths BUSTED!

It's worth pointing out that while there are many other channels, we're focusing on three because Facebook, LinkedIn, and Google make up 95% of the effective ROI-producing spend that we manage across accounts at Right Percent. Fourth and fifth place are so far behind, they aren't even worth mentioning in this context. I also bring this up to point out that **channel expansion beyond the big three is NOT a major lever.** This is a common misconception that goes back to the idea of spreading your bets across ten channels. Expanding to minor channels could be a minor brand play, but it's never an ROI-producing lever in the sense we're talking about here.

Another harmful channel misconception is that Facebook doesn't work for B2B. That's blatantly not true. Facebook works great, but you need a certain audience size. My rule of thumb is 200,000 decision-makers.

People underestimate how power laws work on channels. Instead of spreading yourself too thin, focus on one or two channels until you achieve maturity. By then, if you've answered the questions outlined in the first part of this book, you should already have a sense of which ones to prioritize. A common mistake is testing too broadly, which dilutes your impact. How do you know when you've reached maturity? You have account maturity when you're spending money and making it back and generally generating legitimate customers from that channel. When you're testing a channel, you should be able to find, within an order of magnitude, whether you have product market fit. It should take no more than $20,000 of testing over three months. And that doesn't mean spending $20,000 at a time. You're spending $1,000 at a time when you're starting and getting iterative feedback as you go.

What I mean by order of magnitude is this: If your breakeven point is $100 per qualified lead, and your initial campaign testing shows the cost per lead to be $500, you can work on optimizing that to $100 per lead within the same basic campaign structure. But if the cost per lead is an order of magnitude higher—that is, over $1,000 per lead—then you should just scrap that approach and try something totally new.

The Power of LinkedIn Ads

Robust targeting

LinkedIn is the one ad platform on the internet built for really robust B2B targeting. The biggest difference between LinkedIn and Meta or Google is that LinkedIn has all the native data: Where someone is working, their job title, how long they have been at a company. And the users are the ones supplying that info and because they use the platform for professional networking and job hunting, that info tends to be up to date. Whereas plenty of people are on Facebook every day but never update their profile. Another important B2B advantage on LinkedIn is that people tend to be in more of a work mindset when they're browsing LinkedIn just because of the nature and focus of the platform. It's where people go to give and get career advice, share work wins, and post work-related content. Someone already in that mindset who sees an ad that can help them improve their job performance might be more likely to engage than if they encountered it on Facebook. The main thing is being able to target the right person.

Hands on (in good ways and bad)

Now, with all the advantages of highly specific manual targeting comes the downside of having to do more work on your part. With Meta/Facebook, you throw a bunch of audiences into the campaign and let the algorithm do its thing. The algorithm will find your leads and achieve the targeting goals you set for it.

With LinkedIn, you have to be fully hands-on to get the most out of its targeting options. You can do targeting along all sorts of parameters, but you can't do them all at once, so you have to test manually to find which audiences engage the most and break large audiences into smaller ones to fine-tune your signal. This is all on you, whereas other platforms do the work for you. On LinkedIn, you have to control the targeting and bids manually.

But that's a good thing in a lot of ways because it gives you total control over the process as opposed to spending a bunch of money on a broad, algorithmically-targeted audience without really knowing which common denominators are driving the leads. If it turns out that those leads were no good, I don't have a good way to fine-tune the way I do with LinkedIn. So, more levers means more work, but it also means more options. and those options give you the power to be next-level specific with your targeting.

Maximum Delivery (Don't do it)

LinkedIn has another targeting option they push called "Maximum Delivery." It's a bad idea for a number of reasons and not something I would recommend. One of the biggest disadvantages of Maximum Delivery is that it does everything on CPM bidding. LinkedIn is really expensive on a CPM basis, it's just not built for that. The "maximum" of Maximum Delivery means maximum impressions. In practice, you'll pay a premium to deliver a ton of ads whether or not they get clicks. If you go with manual bidding, and you should on LinkedIn, you'll run on a cost-per-click basis and only pay when someone actually clicks on your ad. Doing it this way works with the native advantages of the platform rather than against them.

Why is LinkedIn so expensive?

LinkedIn would never put it this way, and it probably isn't their intention, but they effectively have a monopoly in what they do because they're the only show in town. There is no better B2B database out there, and nobody else is collecting self-supplied user information that can be used for targeting, in the same way. They don't have a monopoly on B2B ads by any means, but of all the platforms, theirs is the closest to a purpose-built B2B ads ecosystem. There are trees all over the world, but only one Amazon Rainforest.

In B2B ads jargon, LinkedIn is a place for firmographic targeting, using all the data employees and employers input on the platform. Put another way, some platforms force you to go looking for a needle in a haystack, with or without algorithmic assistance. LinkedIn lets you pick your needle from a well-organized stack of needles.

Getting started on LinkedIn

Targeting

Once you know who you're targeting and have answers to all those important background questions, it's time to set up a targeting structure based on your target audience: only people in finance or only tech with a company size of 20-50 employees. You can also target companies based on revenue—whether it's pre-revenue startups, high-revenue enterprises, or anything in between.

Creative and offer

After that, once you have your ad creative, you set up your lead form for your offer whether that's a demo, a sales meeting, or a trial.

Let it rip

Once you have your lead form together and your ads are good to go, it's time to just launch and go.

With other platforms, you'll let the algorithm do its thing at this point, but with LinkedIn, you're going to be adjusting bids manually. Just remember, it's going to be expensive. Stay smart and strategic. Don't get freaked out by the figures. LinkedIn will suggest a bid, usually between $10-15 at the time of this writing. You'll say okay, I want to bid $11 per click. Then you see what happens and adjust accordingly.

Control

I know I might sound like a broken record at this point, but the name of the game on LinkedIn is control. You'll see a bunch of options like Maximum Delivery, which we've covered, and Cost Cap, which lets you set a maximum bid for a conversion. But your best option is manual bidding. Unlike Google, LinkedIn is not going to charge you the lowest possible price to get in front of somebody. You have to take the reins and understand the implications of outbidding your budget.

You'll know you're on the right track when you're consistently delivering about 98-99% of your budget. That would tell you that your bid is exactly right for your audience. Anything more than that, and you're overpaying. On other platforms, this is not something you can control or something you have to worry about. LinkedIn gives you this lever. Use it wisely.

Beware of "or" statements

One thing to watch out for when you're setting up your targeting is using a lot of "or" statements. These can broaden your search too much and undercut the value of specific targeting. If you're looking for someone in finance *or* tech, then you're not being specific enough. You're targeting everyone in finance and everyone in tech, whereas someone who works in finance AND tech is a very specific target.

Don't overdo it

The opposite problem is going too narrow. You might be tempted to use strict controls to get down to a tiny pool of people. Maybe you see an audience of 5,000 and think, oh, that's exactly the 5,000 people I want to target. That's probably not the case. You're better off broadening from that original 5,000 to include 50-100,000 or more. Between the cost and algorithmic limits of LinkedIn, it's hard to optimize well within a group of 5,000, where 50,000 is more manageable.

Strategic Takeaways

LinkedIn provides strong B2B targeting, using self-supplied professional data to reach specific audiences.

- Robust targeting: LinkedIn leverages up-to-date, self-reported professional data to deliver precise B2B targeting that outperforms general platforms.
- Manual control: Unlike algorithm-driven platforms, LinkedIn requires advertisers to actively manage targeting and bids for optimal campaign performance.
- Cost-effective bidding: Avoiding the costly "Maximum Delivery" CPM option in favor of manual CPC bidding ensures better control and cost efficiency.

The Magic of SEM (Google)

Even Google doesn't know how Google works

A big caveat before we get into SEM (search engine marketing) or paid search, aka Google. So much of how Google functions is hidden behind a black box that even Google doesn't fully understand the inner workings of. Nothing we cover in this section or anywhere else pretends to know how Google exactly works or where they're going. But we don't need to know that to use Google effectively. Our search best-practices are grounded in doing what works and constantly iterating. It's an evergreen methodology. Whatever changes happen behind the curtain, operating this way will allow you to adapt and keep doing what works.

Google keeps us in business

When I say that Google is a big part of the reason us agency folks still have jobs, I'm not just talking about the share of our work that paid search makes up, which is substantial. The real job security for people like the Right Percent team is in knowing how to implement the best practices that Google makes freely available. If you want to read them, Google puts out all these documents on how to run ads on their platform. The thing is, these assume you have all the resources and knowledge to actually implement these tactics and, as we cover in this chapter, the experience to know when to deviate from conventional wisdom as spelled out in the latest tutorial. Google's insights are great, but they are a case of "the map is not the territory." To understand SEM best practices in . . . well, practice, you have to account for all sorts of internal factors Google doesn't mention, like the strengths and weaknesses of your internal team (and/or the team you hire), your tracking and development capabilities beyond just Google's own reporting, and your propensity for risk.

The day Google releases a comprehensive guide detailing exactly what to do, how to do it, how each lever influences your actions, how to measure success, what to do if things aren't working, how to scale when they are, and how to pivot when you've exhausted your keywords—that's the day we'll be out of work, and this section of the book will become obsolete. Until that time, we're happy to help and share what we've learned along the way.

High intent = low-hanging fruit

When building a search account from scratch, start with the highest intent, lowest-hanging fruit. To use Brightwell, the B2B childcare SaaS company, as an example, terms like "childcare management software" are highly relevant.

Google is an auction-based, pay-per-click model. So, you tell Google more or less what you want to show up for. The match types you select will dictate how much liberty you want to give Google in terms of close variance or similar themed searches. Simply put, you're saying, *I want to show up for these terms, and I'm willing to pay $X*. From there, it's an auction. What you're bidding, combined with your quality score, is going to dictate where you show up on the page and when someone clicks on your ad.

Is your page Las Vegas or Boise, Idaho?

Quality Score is Google's signal for user experience. Basically, did users have fun on your page or get what they wanted when they clicked? If users consistently bounce back to search from your landing page, that signals lower quality to Google. If your landing page copy closely matches what your ad says you're all about, that boosts your relevance and, therefore, your quality score. The more you can signal to Google that your page provides a relevant and high-quality user experience, the cheaper your ads will be on Google.

It's also critical that you align your offer with what users are searching for. All of this might sound obvious, but you'd be surprised how many companies don't get this. So, if they're searching for childcare management software, your ad is going to want to speak directly to that with some sort of value proposition offer or incentive that will connect with those users. Put yourself in their shoes and give them something worth finding.

Sticking with our daycare management software example, a more mid-funnel or upper-funnel search term might be "daycare management." It's relevant, but they haven't specified they're looking for software. This searcher is less likely to be as motivated or ultimately to convert. This user is in the consideration phase, they might be looking for tools, but they're not looking specifically for your product. You go after this stuff only after the bottom funnel stuff has shown a conversion signal with a path to a demo, signup, or whatever your offering.

Saturation—or—scrapping the bottom of the funnel

All good things must end, and high-intent search terms are no exception. What ends up happening with search is you tap out your bottom-of-funnel, high-intent stuff. As you can imagine, there's only so many people out there searching for childcare management software. So, you have to start expanding the radius of users you're reaching. You could try a few things like changing the core term. Instead of "childcare . . . " try "daycare . . . " or "preschool management software." Expand that bubble to tangentially related terms. And once you tap those out, aim higher in the funnel.

Your creative will need to follow those changes, so adapt your copy and landing pages accordingly.

Intent alignment

Speaking of landing pages . . . If your ads are just sending people to your homepage, you're missing out. Instead, you can be way more optimized by breaking out subsets and aligning their intent, in terms of search language and the outcome they're ultimately searching for with where you send them.

If you know they're searching for "childcare app", why would you send them to your homepage? Wouldn't they be better served and more likely to convert if you directed them to a demo of the app or a landing page that speaks to its merits?

If someone's searching with "cost" in their term, why not send them to a pricing page.

Those considerations when you're structuring your account can pay dividends when your campaign is live.

3 types of keywords

Head term
Every business has a core, what we call a "head term." This could be "insurance quotes" for an insurance company or "attorney + YOUR CITY" if you're a lawyer. These are high-converting. That's your non-brand beachhead.

YOUR BRAND NAME HERE
Brand keywords are self-explanatory. The general rule is that if other companies are bidding on your brand name on search, you have to bid to protect yourself. It's a bit of a protection racket from Google. We've tested this multiple times for multiple clients, and you really do lose business if you don't bid on your own brand terms.

Competitor
This means bidding on your competitors' brand names. Generally, someone searching for a close competitor is likely to be qualified for your product. The big issue is that they may not have intent to switch. This is why competitor bidding can really be optimized with custom landing pages and ad text, telling users why they should consider switching to your brand.

Overview of the three keyword types

The reason to separate these is because they require different strategies and perform differently. That's why you don't want to lump these categories together. Brand tends to perform best because there are no higher-intent searches out there. People are looking for you already, it doesn't get better than that. However, there are all sorts of questions around incrementality with branded search. The big issue is how much you want to pay.

Non-brand search will have your highest volume, depending on the category and the vertical. It may not be your highest-converting or where you put most of your spend, but in terms of the universe of keywords, there's just more out there in this category. Ultimately, non-brand is where most accounts are going to focus because they won't exhaust non-brand as quickly as branded keywords.

Competitor depends on a lot of factors not directly related to ad metrics, like where you are in your niches in relation to your competition, how fiercely you want to go after them, and how much it would cost to do so. It's also a question of the space you take up in the minds of your audience, which is ultimately a branding question. The main thing to know here is that best practices are similar to brand but in reverse, and that doing this right involves a lot of research and competitive analysis.

Quality leads? Search no further . . .

SEM is unique among B2B marketing channels in that you're not using it to reach a cold audience. You serve ads to people who are looking for the things your business offers. People are hand-raising. They're coming to you. And that's why SEM typically has the best quality traffic of any channel.

Search is more demand capture than it is demand generation. On paid social, LinkedIn, or even YouTube, you're paying to get in front of a demographically and/or firmographically targeted audience that's presumably interested in what you have to offer. You can think of search as more of a bottom of the funnel activity. They're looking to buy, and you're selling.

Go broad only when you have a conversion signal (no matter what Google says)

"Google's own best practices will generally tell you to go broad (their word) on keywords. On the surface, this seems to make sense. Something super broad like "real estate Portland" could get you other real estate and Portland-related things, like "Portland Realtors" and real estate listings for the suburbs of Portland.

I like to tell people to avoid those broad keywords because it can get really hairy in terms of pulling in all sorts of irrelevant things you don't want. Instead, I suggest going broad only when you have a conversion signal. If you have that, those broad keywords can work well."

—Luke Roshon, Director of B2B Demand Generation at Right Percent

If you're targeting something way down-funnel like a purchase, or if you're passing qualified lead data back into Google, broad keywords can help you optimize the search terms that are more likely to generate that qualified lead you want to make that purchase. But if you don't have super down-funnel conversion action, which is pretty standard in B2B, or if you're just going off of a more upper funnel event, like a lead, you're better off controlling your search terms more tightly. There's more power in phrasing in exact match, especially if you don't have the right data passing back up to feed the algorithm targets.

"Google loves to tell you to lean heavily on their own automation with broad keywords and just let them optimize. And that definitely works if you have a good conversion signal. Meaning you integrated your CRM with your ad platform with all the dev work to pass back offline conversion to the platform.

'But we don't have that,' you say . . .

This is where businesses go wrong following Google's advice. They go broad and optimize for top-of-funnel MQLs and, surprise, surprise, the quality is garbage. They're implementing the right practices, but without the gunpowder to make it happen."

—Derek Hoffman, Director of Growth Marketing at Right Percent

Our first question isn't to go broad or not to go broad. We try to take a diagnostic approach before we start writing prescriptions. None of the advice we have to offer is a one-size-fits-all blanket statement for every SEM account. If we go back to sending users to a landing page instead of your homepage . . . that's not advice we give out of context. What we suggest is for high-volume, non-brand search, you should have dedicated, intent-aligned pages.

But what if you don't have the in-house or freelance talent to turn out those pages? Fine.

Scratch that, let's direct everyone to the homepage, but – and here's the part Google won't tell – let's optimize for Closed Won deals, or Sales-Qualified Leads instead of Marketing-Qualified leads.

But what if you don't have the dev resources for that?

It's okay, there are workarounds. . . .

SEM is always a tailored solution. Google's best practices only work in laboratory conditions with unlimited resources. If that's you, do what they say to the letter: focus on conversion signal, focus on onsite experience, go for conversion rate, and conversion signal. You'll do fine. You can do all sorts of things in search and in life with unlimited resources.

The rest of us need to be smart and find the workarounds.

What does a good conversion signal look like?

A good conversion signal is something that is aligned with your revenue event. If you think about a multi-step B2B funnel, there are a few steps between the initial click and a closed lead. Some are on-site, like clicking the form on a landing page, which qualify as MQLs, and there are other funnel steps that give you SQLs. And you're going to have drastically different conversion rates from MQL to CW based on the keyword set, device type, and a host of other factors.

Now, this is where we run into problems with Google best practices again because at this stage, you're bound to have quality issues if you value all those MQLs the same because Google and most platforms do a really good job at driving leads but a really poor job of driving high-quality leads. Therefore, you're looking at a world of difference if you're able to optimize for MQL vs SQL, and there's a difference between having the reporting for that and then also having the reporting on the platform. If you have the reporting on the backend and it's not integrated, meaning you're not passing information back to Google, then you can manually manipulate that MQL and say, okay, well, 'Campaign A' MQLs are only worth $50, but 'Campaign B' MQLs are worth $100 because I know they have twice the down-funnel conversion rate.

You can also feed it back information and just say, *forget MQLs, we're optimizing for SQLs. And, while you're at it, use smart bidding*. Then, Google will do all that automatically. That approach cuts the manual work and allows you to be more broad and more liberal in your targeting approach.

Match type and keyword intent

There's a lot that goes into a match type strategy on paid search, but the most important is this: An exact match means showing up for the exact of a given search phrase. Broad match is like a big net.

Broad is fine if you're optimizing on the platform for SQLs, but not for MQLs. The issue being that Google will send you broad matches all day, and those users won't convert. But the better the conversion signal you have, the broader you can go.

Keyword type

We've covered middle and upper funnel keywords. With SQL tracking, Google can find users with a wider net using middle funnel terms and still bring you relevant matches. That never used to be the case, back in the manual days. However, smart bidding has changed the game, but you can really only unlock effective smart bidding with a strong conversion signal. Now it's a matter of knowing which conversion signal you're after and having the resources to implement it.

Google and the "E"-word

Which conversion signal to use comes down to quality vs. volume. It's the classic algorithm problem of garbage in/ garbage out. If you want to train the algorithm to go after a good signal, you need a good signal to train it on. So, that's quality. But the second piece of that puzzle is having enough volume. If you decide you're going to optimize for CW, five of those a month isn't going to be enough to use.

There's a difference between what Google says is enough and what is actually enough to really tell you something useful. Over time, Google has needed less and less conversion volume to the point where their most recent guidance suggests something like 15 conversions per month or thereabouts across the account. That is such low data. Again, this is a place where no best practices sheet or knowledge base is going to give you the exact right answer, and what's really needed is human experience to navigate the grey area. "Enough" isn't a binary you either have or you don't. It's a scale where 15 might work or it might not.

Basically, the more volume you have, the quicker you can make a decision. I would call this "account velocity." If you came to me and asked, "how are the tests going? Do we need to change this or that? Should we change bidding?" and you only had 15 conversions per month, I would say you shouldn't be doing anything. At that scale, you should be making decisions over a couple of months because you need the algorithm to ingest that information. Now, if you were a big e-commerce platform getting thousands of conversions per day, then, yeah, get after it and make those changes immediately. See what the change does and respond accordingly.

"But what if I don't wanna wait?"

As a rule, the more data, the better. And, if you are on the lower end of the scale, that means waiting until you have enough for meaningful analysis. But if you're restless and want to be hands on and manage your account in a very active way, you either need to refocus your strategy to one that works for that style of management, or you need to learn some patience and accept that you can't make changes every day without the volume to back them up.

But Google doesn't tell you this, and, until now, you won't find it in any book. Google says you only need 15. But some simple math and common sense can tell you how small that number really is and give you some much-needed perspective. You're talking less than one conversion per day across your entire account.

Impression share

Usually, impression share comes up when you're trying to improve or grow an existing account rather than build one from scratch, which is mostly what we've covered up to this point. Account goals are typically one of two things or both. Either they want more volume, they want better Customer Acquisition Cost (CAC), or they want more volume *and* better CAC. In other words, every account wants to grow and be more efficient.

Let's say you have an existing structure and you want more volume: you can get there either through increased impression share—getting more impressions on the terms you are bidding on, which you can achieve either through a higher budget or by improving your quality score. Budget is the lowest-hanging fruit because if you're not constrained by budget, this is dead easy. Increasing your budget won't mess with your bid because, the way Google works, you're simply saying that you're willing to spend more if there's more to be had. The other option is to bid more, but the downside of this is it drives up your cost. If you're willing to pay more per click, your impression share will go up, but so will your CPC.

100% impression share and its limits

With brand keywords it is possible to own or try to own 100% impression share. That's rare with non-brand. But let's say that's what you're working with. One of two things will happen: You're going to run out of impressions, or you're going to hit your CAC guardrail. So, most companies with performance marketing say they're not willing to pay more than $1,000 per new customer or whatever their number is. Now, either one of those things is bound to happen. Your conversion rate is going to be phenomenal, but this won't last. An 800-pound gorilla, growing and running out of space, may start bidding on your brand name. This can happen even faster when you're in a vertical of your own or a tight duopoly. Eventually, with enough companies bidding on your name, it usually becomes impossible to keep to CAC guard rails at 100% impression share. A typical ad account brand campaign is most efficient around 90% impression share, but this number will change for different clients.

Peak CAC

CAC, in this dynamic, is kind of like peak oil. We're never going to actually run out of oil, because we'll run into the prohibitive costs of extracting the last drops (or burn the atmosphere) before we actually run out. The same law of diminishing returns tells us that most marketers run into their CAC constraints long before they hit impression share constraints (or 100% impression share).

This works like a curve. The higher you get on the demand curve for impression share, the more expensive those clicks become. And, make no mistake, you will run into this very quickly.

Incremental costs vs total costs

The best way to think about those guardrails is in terms of incremental costs rather than total costs. At first, doubling your conversions might take you from $1,000 to $2,000. But the next jump, to generate just one more conversion, might take $10,000. This kind of bidding becomes unsustainable very quickly.

An account working out the numbers might say they can afford to go from $300 per conversion all the way up to $4,000 based on their unit economics. But then they look at their data and say, *hey, actually, we can generate another conversion per week*. This makes sense to do, so they bump up the budget they can spend because they're still under $4,000. But the next bump isn't going to be worth it. They'll have reached the point where it's no longer profitable to chase impressions, even though there's still impression share to be had.

Growth opportunities

Now, imagine doing everything we've covered here across all your campaigns or all your ad groups. This is the kind of thing I'm talking about when I contrast "laboratory" ad conditions with how things go down in the real world. One group might be running above your CAC constraints, so you should be bidding that down. Another might be over, so bid that up. That's the basic grammar of optimization theory. It's the art and science of reallocating budget to its highest-valued use.

Once everything's optimized and on a level playing field, you can increase your impression share either via bid or quality score.

There's a lot of ambiguity around quality score, and some of it is opaque and known only to Google, but think of it as a measure of your relevance. It's in Google's best interest not to deliver a shitty experience. Let's say your CMO is tripping off his or her rocker and wants to sell T-shirts using childcare management software terms. That's not against the rules; they're allowed to bid on that, but Google is going to deem you low-quality because Google knows that someone looking for childcare management software is gonna have a bad time if they find your stupid, irrelevant T-shirts instead of the SaaS solution they're looking for.

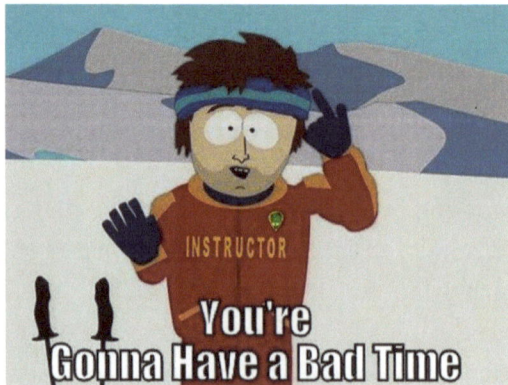

That's an extreme example, but you could think about it on a micro-scale in relation to intent alignment. The difference between "preschool," "daycare," and "childcare" as mixed and matched with "pricing"

or "app" could all yield very different quality scores depending on the relevance of your copy to those search terms.

A word of caution, and I can't believe this needs saying in 2025 . . . But none of this is to say you should go around keyword stuffing. That hasn't worked in over a decade. Google doesn't spell out exactly how they determine quality, but things like click-through-rates, dwell time, and bounce rates all play into it. These aren't metrics you can fudge by loading up on empty keywords. Google's too smart for that, so come correct with value, relevance, and a good user experience.

Volume and net new inventory

You increase click volume through net new inventory. This goes back to keyword types, keyword categories, and keyword sets. When you go from bidding exact to throwing a wider net based on a good conversion signal, there's net new inventory to be had based on terms, placements, geo language, and other factors. Unlike some of the other levers that can help you move the SEM needle, there's nothing nebulous here. It's very straightforward.

Suppose you weren't bidding on mobile before because it wasn't converting, but now you have a better converting mobile page, so you decide to open that up. Boom! Net new inventory.

You weren't bidding in Canada before?

No Spanish terms?

These could all be blue oceans of fresh inventory.

The difference 10% can make

Let's say you get a 10% improvement in conversion rate. That does two things for you:

First, it improves conversion volume and your efficiency by 10% overnight on everything that you're doing, assuming that it was a universal change. Suddenly, your CAC is 10% lower than it was before.

Now, it's time to revisit the demand curve and examine what you can do with the ability to bid up by 10% without overrunning your guardrails.

A word about the auction

Google is a competitive auction. We've covered what this means in terms of strategy and how your payback time influences your competitiveness.

What allows you to compete are two main things:

Life Time Value (LTV)

What are you getting? What's your value per click as expressed in the lifetime value of a conversion? That is determined by the value of your down-funnel conversions and your mid-funnel conversion rates. Those can be two different things depending on if you are cross-selling or upselling in different funnel stages. These can impact your LTV and, consequently, what you can bid, which in turn drives more volume.

Mid-funnel conversion rate

Maybe you found a better sales process, or you improved a landing page and got your 10% boost that way. That is not going to increase the value of your bottom goal, but it is going to increase the number of conversions you get, which increases the value-per-click. So, an increase of a 1% or 2% conversion rate would allow you to increase the maximum value-per-click from search ads from $20 to $40.

Impression share AKA the 800-pound gorilla

The value of your LTV and your conversion rate dictate your ability to compete. This ends up relating to impression share and the 800-pound gorilla problem. At some point, factors like brand recognition and brand trust will impact your ability to convert those clicks, and once again, we're out of the lab and dealing with how this all plays out in real life. This is a harsh reality for David when he optimizes and does all the right things but is up against a Goliath at the auction. All else being equal, assuming they've done everything we suggest to a 'T', an upstart shoe company loses to Nike every time.

But because there's nothing the underdog can do to control this dynamic, they just have to accept it and focus on what you can control:

monetizing your leads better, improving your conversion funnel, and brushing up on your slingshot skills.

Strategic Takeaways

- Opaque but adaptable: Google's SEM operates like a black box where success comes from relying on evergreen best practices and continuous iteration rather than complete transparency.
- High-intent targeting: SEM captures quality, high-intent traffic by aligning ad messaging and landing pages with users' specific search queries and conversion signals.
- Smart auction dynamics: Effective SEM requires mastering bidding strategies and balancing quality score, conversion volume, and lifetime value to optimize cost efficiency.

Meta-Facebook & Instagram Ads for B2B

Why Facebook targeting is counterintuitive

There's a paradox when it comes to targeting on Facebook. With most ad platforms, you're trying to go as targeted as possible, whether that's through retargeting based on their interests, a lookalike audience, or other insights into exactly who is likely to connect with your ad. Facebook is the same, but different. The process is reverse-engineered. You start with the conversion action you want and supply enough information for Facebook to do the targeting. As a rule, we suggest keeping your hands off the controls, with the exception of geo-targeting. Of course, you do want to limit your ad to the regions and areas your business serves. But other than that, you're better off letting Facebook handle the targeting.

Your main task is to rotate creative and test a lot of creative to find what works with those broader audiences.

"The targeting methodology on Facebook is pretty much the exact opposite of LinkedIn. These are broadly targeted campaigns where best results come from selecting no targeting parameters at all. Your goal is to build a conversion signal and train Meta's algorithm to find the right people."

—Joe Lester, Performance Marketing Lead at Right Percent

Conversion signal is everything on Facebook

A strong conversion signal is important regardless of platform, but on Meta, it's everything. At the most basic level, it might be somebody going to your site and filling out a lead form from an ad on Meta. As you gain more conversions and more data, you want to feed the algorithm a higher-quality signal, so you're not just looking for somebody who downloaded a demo, but someone who downloaded a demo and then became qualified by sales. The further you can move down the sales funnel while retaining enough sales data for meta to learn from, the stronger your campaigns will be.

Let the algorithm ride

If you take away just one best practice for Meta, it is to just "let the algorithm ride," in the words of Right Percent's Joe Lester. We've said it before, and we'll say it again. The algorithm is what sets Meta apart from other channels, and it works best when you let it do its thing. LinkedIn, by contrast, thrives on precise targeting. Google is somewhere in between Meta and LinkedIn. Meta is the extreme end of the spectrum. You target nobody and let Meta find your conversions.

The algorithm thrives on data. The more you feed it, the better it can solve your problem. Meta casts a wide net and trains the algorithm on what it learns from those broad placements.

Junk leads

One corner of Meta that consistently brings in a lot of spam and junk leads are Reels on Instagram and Facebook. There are a lot of potential explanations for this, but the simplest and most likely is that users turn their brains off while they're infinitely scrolling, so they're not in a receptive mindset for a B2B offer, and they're unlikely to stop and read a visual headline and text-based ads. Ultimately, the reason something doesn't work doesn't matter.

If it doesn't work, don't do it. While we've said to cast a wide net and trust Facebook, in practice, you'll soon find there are a few places where the ads it serves bring in low-quality leads. Just cut those and immediately improve your average.

If you choose "all placements," Meta is never going to discriminate. As long as you have a strong conversion signal, Meta will be quick to learn that the sales-qualified leads you're seeking aren't coming from Reels. You could also just uncheck the box to show up in Reels, but the default is using every placement.

Impression share

Impression share is a more nebulous metric on Meta and doesn't carry the same fatalistic weight that it does for our example of the upstart sneaker brand taking on Nike on Google.

The important difference here is that you're not dealing with an auction model where a winner takes (almost) all. Let's say there are a million impressions available and you show up for 700,000 of those available impressions. That's a 70% impression share. But that doesn't tell the whole story because it's not like there's only 30% left over for everyone else to capture. Another company might have 65% impression share of the same audience because Meta is serving up their ads right after yours. Impression share still matters on Meta, but it's very much a case of running your own race and gauging how much of your target audience you're reaching vs. how you're doing relative to the competition.

Broad targeting & First party data

The best Facebook campaigns really nail broad targeting. They effectively address the paradox we mentioned earlier by having ads that are very targeted and optimized for a given conversion signal but run in a broad way that trains the algorithm and lets Facebook work its magic.

The other way to make it work is to feed Meta first-party data. You can either target them directly or build lookalike audiences with it.

For targeting directly, if you use a tool like 6Sense or ZoomInfo to generate a list of leads, you can easily upload and target those leads on the Facebook ad platform. This is an important part of any Account Based

Marketing campaign, where you target the same accounts throughout the web.

Lookalikes are a little more complex but still easy to test. Say you have a list of 5,000 contacts, people who you know are quality and qualified. What you can do with that data is retarget and reach them directly, or you can build a lookalike audience. You take those 5,000 people to Meta and say, find me more like these. You'll probably end up with an audience of a few hundred thousand up to a couple of million people who Meta thinks are similar, and you can use that audience to target.

Both of the above targeting types are generally inferior to pure algorithmic targeting on Facebook, but they can work.

Advantage Plus Audiences

Meta has a product called Advantage Plus Audiences that allows you to plug in your first-party data and lookalikes, and Meta will find those people first but will include others outside of that audience who look similar and seem likely to convert. It's a way of putting guardrails on broad targeting and letting Meta know what you kinda want your audience to look like. It's not right for every campaign, but Advantage Plus Audiences are an interesting way to bring a lot of data to Meta and target in a way that makes sense of it all.

Don't forget product-market fit

Any business investing heavily in performance marketing, including Meta and LinkedIn, needs to ask themselves: *do we have product-market fit?* before jumping into ads.

For all their advantages, ads are a bad way to determine product-market fit. If you don't know whether you have it, it's going to be very hard to find high-quality leads because you'll have no metrics for quality. You'll be taking performance out of performance marketing. The advantage of performance marketing is that you're training the algorithm. You define the people you're looking for and trust the algorithm to go find more of them for you to target directly. And you have to know that these people want what you have and that your product works for them before you jump into this.

This holds true across all platforms, but Facebook is the channel that will call attention to a lack of product-market fit most spectacularly. On Facebook, you're reaching a cold audience without factors like intent and demographic/firmographics that may allow you to get lucky up to a point on another platform.

Strategic Takeaways

- For B2B on Meta, broad targeting and minimal manual controls let Facebook's algorithm optimize for conversions rather than relying on hyper-specific audience targeting.
- Prioritizing strong conversion signals, creative testing, and first-party data empowers Meta to learn which audiences deliver quality leads while weeding out low-performing placements.
- Utilizing features like Advantage Plus Audiences alongside ensuring solid product-market fit is key to achieving effective and scalable ad performance.

Strategy

Postmortem questions following an underperforming campaign

I try not to say "failed" campaign, because it's not a failure if you learn from it. If you're doing a postmortem on an ineffective campaign or you're auditing a generally chaotic approach to ads that isn't producing the results you want, you should be looking for your blind spot. What questions didn't you ask going into the campaign that could have informed a different approach?

The two most consistent blind spots that can sink a campaign are:

1. Not having leading indicators built into the campaign.

Remember that B2B marketers need to create LIFE – "Leading Indicators of Future Earnings." This means when a lead comes in, you want to be able to approximate its value. You use the qualifying questions you ask in the form or measure the actions those leads take in your funnel—but either way, you need to know the value of those leads as fast as possible in order to make effective decisions. You do this with leading indicators.

2. Not thinking about what you're actually offering

This blind spot is almost inevitable when the content team and the ad team are separate and don't talk to each other. What ends up happening is that the content team makes some content and asks the ad team to put $20,000 on it with social ads. There's no learning or iteration. Nobody's putting money on the content that gets better results and cutting what doesn't.

There's no process of working with the content team to achieve advertising goals. This is another way of saying, start ad campaigns by making sure your offer aligns with the goals of your business and your ideal customer.

Other fatal flaws include not testing enough positioning statements. This tends to be a creative blind spot where the wrong question is, "is this ad perfect?" when you should be asking, "do we have enough positioning statements to test?"

Problems with audience are almost always a result of going too broad or too small. The blind spot is in where you put your trust. If you know you want to reach a small audience, you don't want to trust the algorithm, you want first-party. But if you have a big audience, it's the exact opposite; trust the algorithm. Things go haywire when you mix those up.

B2B Attribution Guidelines

How confident are you in your tracking and attribution?

Most B2B companies can get to a confidence ratio of 75% of their closed leads coming from trackable channels and the other 25% is untracked. That's fine, because you can use the 75% as your guide for what's working and what's not. The way things are tracked historically, there's a lead that comes to the website from an ad, and the ad information is stored in the URL that the visitor came from. It's usually called UTM information, which is an archaism from the early days of Google analytics when Google bought a platform called Urchin Tracking Management. That was 20 years ago, but the acronym stuck, even though it no longer means anything. UTM tags get stored on that customer's record when they submit the lead or start the demo on your website. There are a million ways to set this up, through your own servers or tools like HubSpot, the point is that it's all trackable.

To assess your own confidence in your attribution, there are a couple of ways to go about it. Early on, you want to do manual checking. Check the email address that came through your lead form against all of the emails your sales team is closing successfully. My top tip for early-stage companies is to just do a VLOOKUP of all your leads and a VLOOKUP of all your customers and opportunities and see where your attribution is not doing well.

For mid-stage, tools like HubSpot and Salesforce can do a lot of that for you by pulling in form information and so on.

At bigger stages, you want to rely on your tech people to set this up and your MarOps to run it.

The golden rule of attribution is that you must know where your leads come from and what happens when they come in. This isn't a trade secret or hack, it's the fundamental law of advertising. Without understanding your attribution, you can't do anything. Your misses will be inexplicable, and your wins will be unrepeatable.

First click, multi-click, and more

The point of click-based attribution is to learn from what the user did before they closed. The purpose of the funnel is to learn and gather data that helps you make decisions that affect how you run your campaigns.

First touch—You give credit to wherever the first click came from, wherever the person discovered you. If they found you through non-brand search ads, while looking for HR software, that's their first touch. If it's on LinkedIn and that was the first ad they had seen, that's the first touch.

First touch is very effective as a default prospecting attribution choice because it gives you the most value for you to spend your ad dollars because the first touch is highly incremental.

Last touch—is much less incremental because at that point there may have been several things that persuaded them to type the name of your company into Google and come to you through branded search.

Attribution Best Practices

Attribution window is another time-bound strategy consideration. This one can get heated because it involves assigning credit for a close. There are three types of attribution:

Touch—Whoever touched the customer (not literally I hope) first gets credit. Did they come in through Facebook, search, or ads?

Last-click—The last thing they clicked gets credit for the campaign. So, if someone starts on Facebook but then Googles you, Google gets the credit.

Any-touch or Multi-touch—Sometimes people do this with some sort of in-house model where they assign value based on different rules, but in general, this is a more permissive way of looking at touchpoints.

Assigning credit between channels

For most advertising, the most important thing is first touch. Now, that's not necessarily a known best-practice across B2B, but it makes logical sense, and our experience confirms it. When you're advertising, you're looking for net new customers. They have the highest incremental value to your business. If someone already knows about you and is thinking about purchasing, and your ad gets them over the finish line, that has value, but not as much value as showing a new customer that you are a possible solution to their problems. Again, this theory runs counter to a lot of advice out there. Most incremental marketers will do last touch. The problem with last touch is it gives too much credit to brand search, meaning if you're DoorDash, you're getting that attribution from folks who are searching for the exact word "DoorDash." This means that even if your Facebook campaign is getting restaurant owners interested in signing up with DoorDash, search will get the credit when they Google your brand name, even though that wouldn't have happened if they hadn't seen you on Facebook first.

The other problem with last touch is that besides the brand search issue, it ends up being a less incremental step in getting someone to come to you because they may have come from any source, so ultimately you end up in an any touch paradigm, which doesn't work unless you have a system to measure it.

Making multitouch work

Just for fun, let's take a second to summarize what effective multitouch attribution looks like. Should you want to go that way, you will need platform-specific technical assistance that's outside the scope of this chapter and this book, but here's what it looks like in theory.

You would start with a big data export from your CRM that looks at each of your customers' touch points, giving you a sense of where people are interacting with your business.

Are they downloading forms from Facebook? How many forms? Are they coming from LinkedIn? Do they find you through SEO articles?

All of this is very valuable knowledge, regardless of your attribution strategy. The next thing is to get all of that info summarized and abstracted, even if you can't use it as a formal acquisition model. Then, if you have enough data, an engineer can take it all and build out an attribution model. Now, you can tell if someone touches Facebook three times, LinkedIn three times, and Google three times, each of them gets a third of the credit.

Again, I spell this out as a theoretical exercise. In practice, it takes a big company with a heap of data to pull that off.

Strategic Takeaways

- Learning from missteps: Analyze underperforming campaigns by identifying blind spots—such as missing leading indicators and misaligned offers—to inform smarter future strategies.
- Robust attribution is essential: Establish reliable tracking (using UTMs, manual checks, and integrated tools) to confidently attribute at least 75% of leads and guide decision-making.
- Attribution methodology matters: Prioritize first-touch attribution for acquiring new customers while exploring multi-touch models to accurately distribute credit across channels.

Testing

Apples to apples

A lot of people have the wrong idea about testing for creative when they're not used to it. Some companies think that when they put creative live on Facebook or LinkedIn that these platforms will serve them evenly and they'll come away with a clean test. So, for instance, you put 10 ads live with $10,000 behind them and each one gets $1,000 of spend. This would allow you to say ad #4 beat ad #2 in an apples-to-apples comparison where one had 300 CPC and the other had 200.

However, because ads run on a power law, it doesn't work that way. If you have $10,000 to spend, one ad will get $9,000, one will get $900, and all the others combined will get $100 and be seen by nobody. So, you don't get clean data. The one with more conversions probably got more spend.

So how do you compare ads against each other within the same campaign or ad set?

Take a look at the ad that got the most spend and then look at the conversion event and see if that highest spending ad is actually getting a good cost-per-conversion. It almost always is because the algorithm is working for you.

Forget about clean testing

You can also do force tests where you split the spending evenly across your ads to see what works. But that's a very costly way to proceed. You may get some manual learning, but the algorithm will be hampered by that, and you'll lose your results overall. And the test will be meaningless when you feed your "winning" ads back into the algorithm.

In general, you have to give up on the idea of clean creative ad tests. Letting Facebook or LinkedIn decide may feel messy, but it's the way to go.

The exception is when you want to learn something specific that's applicable even outside of ads, see below.

Testing outside of ad learning

The exception to giving up on manual learning is when you want to learn something outside of ad learning, like answering an R&D-type question or testing a logo or a tagline. An algorithmic or auction-based ad platform isn't the place for that, and neither is this book.

If we're talking about ad learning, 9 times out of 10, you should just throw a bunch of ads on the platform and let it decide what works.

A/B testing isn't really a thing most of the time in ads

This is another one of those myths this book is designed to bust once and for all. People assume you're talking about A/B testing when you talk about ad testing.

Most of the testing in modern ads is not A/B. So, I just want to make it clear that's not what we're talking about here. The one exception to this, where formal A/B testing does come up, is with brand lift studies (which we don't cover in this book).

So, forget about A/B. Testing, for our purposes, is multivariate testing that relies on the black box of the algorithm to run the test.

Testing best practices

For ad testing, it's about getting as many different positioning statements and visual headlines as you can get approved to test different offers and benefits as frequently as possible on your chosen platforms.

We try to get nine new ads every two weeks on a mature ad account with at least $100k monthly paid social spend. This is the process we've found to be most effective.

Priorities

There are a couple of different things you're testing with ads. These are the top two in order of priorities.

1. Low-hanging fruit around the visual headline

Are there any ways of approaching this product you haven't tried?

How do you call out the exact decision-makers, and test different ways to do that for different decision-makers?

Which benefits resonate?

2. Your offer

Which offer is best to make ads for? Should it be an incentive or a content piece?

Spreadsheets won't get you where you need to go

Spreadsheets have had a good run in the world of ad testing, but they don't hold up to the power law when running ads on Facebook and other "black box" platforms where you can't force ad spend. It's hard to plan ahead and say, "we're gonna run this ad in this month" and follow a traditional media buying plan that would fit neatly on a spreadsheet. The other issue is that variables don't apply consistently in the future. Again, due to the black box nature of algorithms, your variables for testing end up being all over the place, and to try and track them would just add friction.

Spreadsheets work for old-school advertising and old-school media buying, but they don't work when you're dealing with the power law and the almighty algorithm.

For example, spreadsheets are great for things like direct mail campaigns where you have complete control of the process and are tracking a limited number of variables.

How to do brand advertising the right way

There are two definitions of brand I want to distinguish before we get into brand strategy as a lever.

The first is brand in the sense of a 'brand advertising campaign, which we've covered before in contrast with direct response ads. A company running brand ads has decided they're either at their limit of their direct response ads, or they don't like direct response ads, so they want to do a campaign to raise awareness of their business.

Generally, the way companies do this is through awareness campaigns to gain a bigger audience—like the stereotypical ads for Coca-Cola that showcase the brand and try to earn a place to live in the consumer's head rent-free. Brand ads showcase the brand but without a clear call to action. In B2C, this can work because of how most people can buy a B2C product. Most people who see an ad for Coca-Cola can buy a Coke in the near future—probably their most famous ad of all time featured a jingle about wanting to "buy the world a Coke."

But in B2B, the percentage of people who are actually able to process your ad and change their awareness is a small segment of the audience. For that reason, these brand campaigns are hard to make work in B2B, and they often fail.

> **The fundamental problem is with targeting**
>
> Companies that run brand campaigns want to unlock new consumers that their direct response campaigns are not reaching, so they want large audiences to serve brand ads to.
>
> On platforms with large audiences - Facebook, Instagram, TikTok, Youtube, etc - the targeting you can select is not good enough to work for B2B on its own.
>
> What makes it work is when you can set up an *algorithmic feedback* loop on a conversion event.

There are a couple of ways around this. One is to still focus on brand awareness, maybe with educational content rather than jingles about peace and love *a la* Coca-Cola in the 70s. But you attach a trackable goal to the campaign, like getting people to download an eBook or some educational content to qualify their interest. Since algorithms recognize engagement, you can use this as an indication that they are a strong lead—someone ideal for your brand campaign—and send that signal back to the platforms. On the other hand, an awareness campaign that goes after some kind of easy content download or something that's trackable can fix the problem of platforms not being able to target your B2B audience for brand effectively.

This is life-or-death for your campaign, because, as we pointed out earlier, if you have no conversion event, the ad platforms (Facebook, You-Tube, etc.) will go after the cheapest users they can get you. Bidding on awareness is a losing game because Facebook tries to get you the lowest cost per thousand impressions (CPM), and that means going after the cheapest, worst people on Facebook that no one wants to target with direct response ads, which is usually not your core B2B audience. On the other hand, if you have a precise audience of 10,000 people that you know are qualified, that your sales team is going after actively, that you've closed business from before, that is a great audience for brand style ads because you don't have the issue of serving the wrong people at auction. You're only bidding on the people you want.

Payback Window Affects Strategy

Your payback window tells you how much you can pay for a new customer. So, if a new customer is going to give you $5,000 in profit or revenue in the next 12 months, then to break even on your campaigns, you need to be spending (all-in, including the sales team) $5,000 or less on average per customer.

This impacts your ad strategy in a few important ways. Generally, the more you can pay, the better you can do at auctions.

This means a lot in search because if someone is willing to accept a 20-month payback and you're only willing to accept a six-month payback and you have the same product and pricing, they can bid nearly four times as much as you on search and basically lock you out of the top parts of the auction. I bring this up again to underscore what a big deal the auction is on both sides of the equation. If there's multiple people in that dynamic, you won't be able to compete in search at all.

Your payback window also impacts how aggressively you go after customers.

If you have a short payback, there's less room for error. You have to get that bread or perish.

None of this is to say that a short payback window is a bad idea. A company that is bootstrapped and focusing on profit is definitely going to want a shorter payback period than a well-funded VC company looking for growth at all costs.

L.I.F.E. or death

Here's the brutal thing about payback. You won't be able to determine payback time until the period's done. You need years of data to get payback. And, as we've made clear, if your payback window is off, you don't have years.

So, before you have that number, you need leading indicators.

Leading indicators are the lifeblood of your B2B strategy, your fuel, your oxygen. You can't do B2B campaigns without them because revenue takes time to be collected and attributed. Leading indicators shorten the time between click and conversion, giving you what you need to feed algorithmic targeting.

Leading indicators give you a prediction of future success, even if you're dealing with a low number of closes at a high value per customer. Leading indicators give you a day-in-day-out sense of what's working, even if that payday is a long way out. Leading indicators let you predict future success accurately while giving you the flexibility needed to run your campaigns.

Strategic Takeaways

- Test smart, not neat: Due to the power law of ad spend, don't expect equal distribution across your ad creatives. Evaluate performance by comparing the highest-spending ad's cost per conversion rather than relying on trying to force even splits of ad spend.

- Tie brand to action: In B2B, brand campaigns must link to trackable conversion events (like content downloads) to avoid serving the wrong audience and wasting ad dollars.
- Plan with precision: Align your strategy with your payback window and fuel it with leading indicators (L.I.F.E.) to forecast future earnings and drive agile, data-informed decisions.

Attribution

Understanding attribution

With most of the accounts we manage at Right Percent, we try to be conservative with what we count as attribution. Generally, we're looking at click-based attribution, where someone has clicked on social or search and gone on to close on the website in a trackable way. I say this is conservative, because there are other attribution models where you would count someone who clicks on Facebook, doesn't sign-up, searches you on Google that night, comes to you through organic, or sees your ads on LinkedIn forever and they finally run into you at a conference and decide to buy. Obviously, that sort of thing exists, but how do you measure it?

4 ways to do measurements

1. Algorithmic testing

Throw your new ads into the algorithm, like we talked about earlier, and figure it out from there. This is the way to go when you have a primarily algorithm-powered campaign for all the reasons we covered earlier about not manually splitting your tests.

2. Traditional A/B testing

This is when you have a set hypothesis to test with two variables you can isolate.

3. Lift testing

Lift tests are like A/B tests, but you're not seeing the exact data. The example we see most often is a geographic lift test. This is the gold standard for brand campaigns. (more on how they're done in the next section)

4. Multivariate testing

This is where you try to collect a variety of data points and use a complicated statistical formula to determine the attribution of your clicks across channels and touch points. B2C at a massive scale can make good use of this (think Amazon massive). But for B2B, you simply aren't going to have enough data points to make it work. We bring it up here only because it's something clients ask about a lot and the answer is always the same. It's not for you.

How to measure geographic lift to test brand campaigns

You run your brand ads to half of your geography, say half the U.S. population. You don't run it to the other half. At the end of the campaign, you see whether the region that saw your ads had higher conversion rates, more closed deals, and whatnot. ChatGPT can help you define your targets and interpret the results of a geographic lift test.

Typically, we run geo lift tests divided by states. You take a list of states and randomize them to run ads on one half and not the other, and see how it affects your overall total sales in those states.

Lift tests work because brand campaigns, by their nature, are not tracked. You're not looking for clicks, you're looking for views and exposure. The only way to measure that is to see what happens to the people who viewed it vs. those who didn't. Geographic lift tests are the cleanest way to do that.

Cross-channel attribution

The only way to truly determine cross-channel attribution is through one of those amorphous split tests, either before and after you start in a channel, or a lift test.

Lift from social

Before and after looks like this: you run Facebook ads for two months and then you pause them for two months and see what happens. You could also do a split test where you stop serving ads to half the country. In either case, you're trying to see how much Facebook is impacting other channels. So, if you turn off Facebook and search goes down 20%, you'll know that Facebook was giving a 20% lift to search. When we run these tests at Right Percent, we tend to see there's a lot of marginal gain that you're not seeing from the account. I've never seen lower than a 15% boost to channels, and I've seen it as high as 100%, with the data to prove it.

The reason for this is that attention-based marketing puts you in front of people who might not even be ad clickers but will go on to search you later. Some research shows that very few Instagram and Facebook users ever click an ad, but that's not to say there's no value to be gained from those people as part of your audience.

Lift from search

On average, there's a big lift from search, but it looks different. Search is usually less incremental. This happens a lot with brand search ads where a lot of people who click your brand ads would have come to your website anyway. They wouldn't have clicked on your competitor's ads. So brand has a lower incrementality and non-brand search is somewhere in between.

First click, multi-click, and more

The point of click-based attribution is to learn from what the user did before they closed. The whole purpose of tracking funnel activities is to learn and gather data that helps you make decisions that affect how you run your campaigns.

First touch

You give credit to wherever the first click came from, wherever the person discovered you. If they found you through non-brand search ads, while looking for HR software, that's their first touch. If it's on LinkedIn and that was the first ad they had seen, that's the first touch.

First touch is very effective as a default prospecting attribution choice because it gives you the most value for the ad dollars you've spent, because first touch is highly incremental.

Last touch

This is much less incremental, because at that point there may have been several funnel steps that persuaded the user to type the name of your company into Google and come to you through branded search.

Any touch

It's more manual, but you can work with a data team to get an export of every touch that your last 500 closed customers had. Get a spreadsheet going that has columns for each touch and go through that manually and get a qualitative idea of where you touched those users.

Then you can crunch the data.

So, if Facebook is in the middle of the funnel for 40% of these . . . that's information you can use to make decisions about how much value to assign to each step of the process.

Working with Other Divisions

Marketing

In theory, the marketing department does marketing, but in reality, marketing is the intersection of a bunch of roles within the company that all have something to do with marketing. This includes the CEO and their vision for the company as expressed through marketing, the product and tech development teams, and design. UX is an important marketing function in PLG companies, and sales is closely tied to marketing in SLG frameworks.

Even within marketing, your ads person or team is going to have to contend with coworkers who may be steeped in some of the myths we've tried to bust in this book, and those people may not see the value of ads or have the wrong idea about how ads work. And for that reason, it's worth thinking of the marketing team as an "other" team when it comes to buy-in around ads.

Tech

Tech is another team with a lot of overlap. Issues like privacy tend to involve legal, marketing, and C-suite input. For example, the question of where your tech team is allowed to place a pixel and what data they're allowed to send back to the platform is a legal concern, but it will also affect marketing goals and workflows. Tech will enable a lot of what you want to do with ads, but they don't operate in a vacuum. Really, none of your teams do, but issues like privacy make overlap inevitable when dealing with tech.

Sales

After tech, the most important team you're working with in B2B is your sales team. Unless you have a completely PLG product, the sales team is driving most of the revenue that comes in. A portion of that revenue is stuff sales is doing on their own— outbound email, attending conferences, etc. But at many B2B orgs, if marketing is doing its job, a lot of what sales does is converting leads that marketing brings in. So, you can think of sales as part of your conversion funnel, which is why it's important to work with them closely.

Working with sales should be a learning experience

Sales knows better than anyone else what actually sells your product to customers. Learn from their experience. Product managers and the tech team might have some insights on this, and can provide data from their analytics about what customers like. But your sales team has to know what their customers want because their livelihoods depend on putting that knowledge into practice. Sales is a great source of information. They'll tell you what benefits customers respond to, what risks seem the biggest to them and what competition you're actually up against. These are great ad insights.

Lead routing

Sales will help you figure out how to effectively route leads. Ask them, and you'll find they have a lot of opinions, but the main thing is you should always be routing leads by lead quality. Sales, more than anyone, want the highest quality leads. Generally, they work with a tier list of leads which may look something like this:

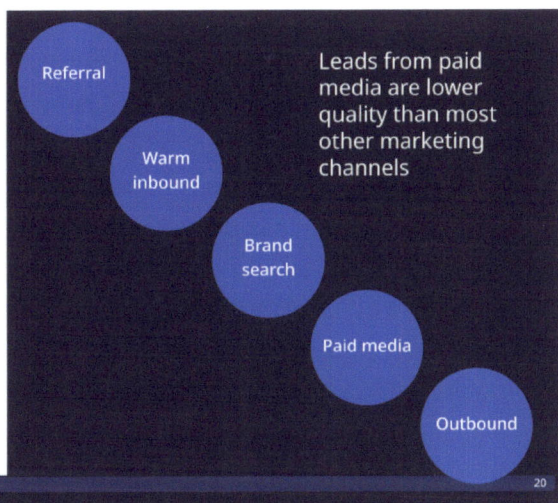

Different types of leads have different levels of intent

Referral
Warm inbound
Brand search
Paid media
Outbound

Leads from paid media are lower quality than most other marketing channels

Right Side Up — 20

Referrals—Arguably the best kind of leads. You can be quite poor at sales and you'll still close that business.

Organic/Direct—These tend to be high-intent, warm leads who have already done their research. The problem with these is that they can spoil your sales team—who are likely to have more of them early on, coming from the founder's network—and they may struggle when it's time to go after lower-intent leads.

Search leads—This is where it gets interesting from an ads point of view. Search leads tend to be higher quality than social leads because they are higher intent. But this is where qualification can make all the difference, because a search lead is not nearly as high quality as leads from further down the funnel, which you can get through the right kind of conversion events.

Ad leads—Almost all leads from advertising are lower intent and generally lower quality. They saw your social ad, they think *hmmm, that seems interesting or valuable*. But they haven't spent much time considering your offer or making a strong decision like filling out a form.

The paradox of scale

The sales team wants high-quality leads, but the business needs to scale, and that usually means getting low-quality leads as well (as a by-product of marketing campaigns) and making the most of them. The best way to deal with this dynamic is to have a "round-robin" system where you rotate sales in and out of a separate team dealing with those lower quality leads from social, paid search, affiliate, and SEO. Not all companies can afford this, but if you can have one or two on your sales team specialize in these harder-to-close leads, it can make a huge difference.

This is where the relationship between marketing and sales becomes crucial. Done right, this can be a key driver of increasing performance from paid ads. But it requires buy-in and teamwork.

Another option is to send leads to the Outbound division of sales, if you have one. Outbound reps are the hardest workers of the sales world, they go out and just reach out to companies with no connection to their own and try to sell to them. If they're doing that successfully, they'll be delighted to work with your leads from ads, because they're so much better than outbound leads. Going back to the tier list, outbound leads are the worst by far. An outbound team is used to doing cold outreach. So, they'll have no problem with leads from social and paid search, and they'll usually kill it.

Legal

The abominable "No" man

Legal could be a division of a bigger company or retained outside counsel at a smaller one. Their whole purpose is to help you avoid legal risk, which means they are incentivized to say "no." If they give the green light, and things go well they get no credit, just their hourly rate. But if they say "yes" and things go wrong, they are finished. And that's a good thing. You want their interests to be aligned with protecting the business from legal exposure. But the default "no" can cause friction when you're seeking legal approval for ad creative.

As we covered in the creative section, the best time to get legal approval is *before* you develop your creative. Get a list of claims and language pre-approved so you're not waiting on legal.

Compliance & privacy

Another area where legal is heavily involved is anything to do with privacy, tracking, and compliance. If you're dealing with GDPR in Europe, this could get very complicated, expensive, and time-consuming. I would recommend getting everyone in a room and making some explicit decisions around cost/benefit analysis.

So, for instance, one of the most contested functions is tracking within the product. So many companies have an unreasonable aversion to this. We won't get into the whole privacy debate here (I have a hot-take on this in a later section), but basically, tracking doesn't mean spying on your customers, and tracking within the product is amazingly helpful for marketers because it can provide a signal that can power campaigns. Some of the best conversion signals come from the product. Working with the tech and legal team to get this approved is really important. There are workarounds if your development people are uneasy.

For one client, we recommended they enable server tracking. The client in question didn't want to track anything because they were scared of legal implications in a heavily regulated industry. We laid out the reasons they should use tracking and presented some ways they could do it without doing anything illegal, unethical, or uncomfortable. The client ended up getting server-side tracking approved, and it boosted their ad performance over 30%.

Campaigns in the Long Term

What if you run a B2B ads campaign and have some success? That's great. But there are two things you should know:

1. **Your work isn't over.** Now it's time to crunch some numbers and study the data to find out what exactly is working and why.
2. **Nothing lasts forever.** You need to know the signs that you're hitting a point of diminishing returns and what to do about it.

Check what's working

What do we mean by success? It means attracting prospects who are likely to generate more revenue than the cost of acquiring them. The first thing to do, when it looks like everything's working, is to check all of your assumptions.

How are you tracking?

Is everything working?

Are as many of the UTMs coming through the URLs of the ad clicks from each channel?

Do these UTMs have the correct campaign, ad set, or ad number on them?

Cohort vintage

A cohort is an arbitrary grouping of leads. For now, let's talk about cohorts by month. So, the January cohort would be all the leads that came in in January.

Vintaging means that more of the leads from a given cohort will be closed to customers over time. So, maybe you close 60% of the January cohort in January, 20% in February, and another 20% over the next six months. This vintaging process is something to pay close attention to. This will tell you if leads are going down the funnel the right way.

What part is driving success?

Another thing to pay attention to when you have a successful campaign on your hands is what element of your campaign is driving that success. This is why iteration is such an important part of everything we do in digital advertising, because it allows you to go line by line through your campaign and find out exactly what is leading to growth.

Diminishing returns

Once you know what's working and how to keep doing it, the next thing is to prepare for audience and ad fatigue. These two forms of exhaustion are the enemies of all B2B advertisers. They're so frustrating because they are inevitable. Unfortunately, all campaigns get worse over time because the audience sees your ads more and more and eventually start to tune them out as ads. One of the biggest levers you have to combat ad fatigue is offering users a variety of content and incentives in your ads.

Gated content **prevents ad fatigue** in B2B ad accounts.

Below is aggregated data. Ad accounts that only use "get a demo" ads and no content ads face headwinds from audience fatigue.

Click Through Rate of Ad Accounts over Time

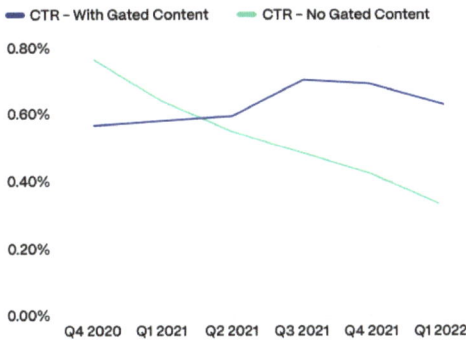

— CTR – With Gated Content   — CTR – No Gated Content

| | Q4 2020 | Q1 2021 | Q2 2021 | Q3 2021 | Q4 2021 | Q1 2022 |

0.80%
0.60%
0.40%
0.20%
0.00%

Local maximum and global maximum

Your local maximum means you're the best locally. It's like being the best at Super Smash Bros in your small town. But then you go to a competition in New York and get smashed. Global maximum is the best in the world. In ads, this can be the difference between a 50% improvement and a 10x improvement.

How do you improve? Not everybody can be the best in the world, but that doesn't mean you can't improve. Once you're sure your tracking is correct, analyze it line by line and come up with plans based on those insights to address the certainty that your audience will fatigue and won't stay the same forever.

All campaigns have a line of diminishing returns

At first, when you're just figuring stuff out, the line on the graph of dollars spent to dollars earned will be all over the place. There's low-hanging fruit to be had, but there's also a learning curve as you create L.I.F.E. But once you have a mature ad account, say you're spending a hundred thousand dollars per month and have been doing so for a year with steady results, there are some things you have to consider. One is fatigue, which we covered, that's a constant battle. The other is scale.

As a rule of thumb, I've observed consistently across clients that if you double the spend of a mature campaign, CAC will go up 50%. So, if you're spending $100,000 each month and your CAC is $1,000, if you go to $200,000 a month, your CAC will increase to $1,500, assuming you make no other changes. You're spending more money to go after the same audience, so naturally your costs will go up per click.

Let's look at Broad on Facebook as an example of how this breaks down. It's roughly the same on every platform. There are 350 million people in America: 75% of them use Facebook, so that's 250 million in your audience. You tell Facebook to find you HR managers, and you qualify those people through all the ways we talked about, the levers of B2B ads. So, Facebook brings you the 500,000 people it thinks are most similar to what you're looking for. Facebook guesses that these are the most likely people to convert. They'll be the cheapest and have the best ROI. When you tell Facebook you want to spend more money to expand the search window, Facebook says, "no problem boss, but we're not going to do that as efficiently as we did with the first 500,000 potential leads. Instead, that'll be $500,000 for the next best 200,000 people." Facebook will proceed to bring you fewer high-quality leads, at least according to the algorithm's estimation (which should be correct if you did everything right). As you spend more, your campaign will get less effective.

This is not obvious to people.

The way this typically plays out: Finance is delighted because a successful campaign is driving ROI down, so they say, "what the hell, let's dump another million in here and really give it a boost."

At this point, I have to tell them we can definitely do that, but unless we change the strategy, adding spend is going to increase our costs.

Checklists for
B2B Ad Performance

B2B Ad Performance

Channel Check	
The three top platforms for B2B ads are Google Search, LinkedIn and Facebook.	
Have you tested Facebook?	☐
Have you tested LinkedIn?	☐
Have you tested Google Search?	☐

All ad platforms	
This advice applies to almost all modern ad platforms.	
Conversion Events:	
Is the conversion event you're optimizing on signifying value to the platforms?	☐

All ad platforms	
Do your ad-sets (or other optimization units) have at least 30 conversions per week?	☐
Does your main conversion event that you optimize on happen within 24 hours of click?	☐
Do you have a tag manager to manage javascript ad platform tags?	☐
Have you implemented server to server events?	☐
Audiences:	
Have you explored targeting with third party audiences? Clearbit, 6Sense, other bought lists?	☐
Do you exclude customers and other low value audiences from your targeting?	☐
Are you targeting the geographies and languages you mean to?	☐

Paid Search	
Paid search for B2B is 85% Google AdWords, 15% Bing.	
Keywords:	B2B keywords are all about establishing both intent and qualification

Paid Search	
Have you explored prospecting keywords based on Terms of Art your customers use?	Terms of Art are phrases that only people in certain professional contexts use. These can be great for B2B, because you know anyone searching for them is likely in your target audience. I.E. A company working in the real-time operations space could use phrases like "Incident Management", "Continuous Delivery", and "On Call Rotation".
Have you explored prospecting keywords based on technical use cases for your products?	This means covering keywords of specific B2B technical use cases that your product or service specifically solves. There are thousands of examples, including terms like "salesforce x integration", "snowflake DB {usage}". If someone uses one of these complementary software, they're likely qualified and interested in your product.
Have you considered bidding on competitor terms?	If there is an 800lb gorilla in your space, its generally worth it to bid on their names and emphasize why you're different.

Paid Search	
Do you review and add negative keywords on a regular cadence?	Negative keywords are important to all AdWords campaigns, but especially in B2B where qualification is key.

Other Search Tactics:

Are you leveraging all applicable ad extensions including image extensions?	Ad extensions provide more inputs for Google to serve and can improve overall ad performance
Search Networks—Are search networks disabled in your account?	Usually a small % of ad spend, but this lower quality traffic is usually reflected in much higher CPAs. Best practice on new accounts is to launch campaigns with this disabled and potentially layer on later as a lower quality growth lever.
Device Bidding—Are you utilizing device bid adjustments to reflect CPA disparities?	B2B accounts typically experience a large disparity between mobile and desktop CVRs. This can be remedied by using smart bidding (tCPA) + a down funnel conversion action that sufficiently aligns with your primary KPI. If you are bidding manually or utilizing tCPA with an upper funnel conversion action, you can remedy the delta with a device type bid adjustment.

Paid Search	
Have you considered scheduling search ads to run when it's most effective for your funnel?	Lead funnels driven by inbound sales often see sizable drops in CVR during off hours due to much longer speed to lead (nights, weekends, and holidays). Smart bidding does not allow DOW/HOD bid adjustments, but you can consider pausing certain days/hours outright or break out campaigns if volume allows. Like device type CVR disparity, this issue can also be addressed by smart bidding + a quality, down funnel conversion action that sufficiently aligns with your primary KPI.
Is your ad copy designed for your target market and relevant to search queries?	Ad copy should reflect the intent if tightly themed ad groups
Are any of your campaigns hitting budget caps?	Short term it is ok to hit budget caps, but long term your campaigns shouldn't be capping out. If they are you should reduce spend by decreasing bids, allowing you to gain efficiency while managing budget.

Paid Social

Paid Social is a key channel for B2B. A lot of best practices are similar between Facebook and LinkedIn, but not all.

Ad Creative and Offer

Does your ad creative contain Visual Headlines that attract your target customer immediately?	The Visual Headline, or text overlaid on the ad image, makes up 60-70% of ad performance. Learn more here.
Are most of your ads in the 1:1 or 4:5 format?	Square ads almost always outperform rectangle ads, which have less page real estate.
Are you testing new creative at least once a month?	The more conversions you have per week and month, the faster ad creative fatigues, and the more you need to test.
If you're a Sales-Led Growth company, are you testing new content at least once a quarter?	For more on Sales-Led Growth vs Product-Led Growth, click here.
Is the content you're promoting laser focused on your target audience?	Content that doesn't meet these two requirements is often hard to use as a conversion tool.
Is the content you're promoting related to your value prop?	☐
Have you tested an incentivized ad, I.E. offering a gift card if the prospect does a demo?	This works shockingly often for driving revenue.

Paid Social

Targeting and Mediums

Have you tested Native Lead Ads?	Leads collected natively on the platform are cheaper but have less intent. About half of our clients find better ROI from Native Lead Ads than on site conversions.
Have you opted out of audience network (On FB and LinkedIn)?	Audience Network on either platform is very rarely a significant percentage of successful campaigns and can drive fraudulent clicks.
(Facebook Only) Have you tested very broad audiences, which can be narrowed down by creative and conversion event?	Facebook has a very strong targeting algorithm—even very narrow, qualified customers can often be best targeted through large "untargeted" audiences.
(Facebook Only) If you use Lead Ads, have you tested Lead Ad filtering?	A new FB feature lets you filter lead ad responders to only ones that are qualified.
(LinkedIn Only) Have you tested narrowing and expanding your target audiences and watching the impact on lead quality?	LinkedIn is less algorithmic, so it's important to test their targeting features thoroughly.
(LinkedIn Only) Have you turned off Audience Expansion?	This is checked by default and is almost always bad for performance.

Reading Your B2B Ad Data

Understanding your B2B ads Data is half the battle

Understanding your B2B ads data is half the battle.	See a full write-up on best practices for B2B ad data here.
Do you know how your conversion events correlate to down funnel revenue?	You should know roughly how much an MQL, SQL, Opportunity is worth to you, as well as product usage statistics.
Do you have cohortized data views?	If a lead came in in January, the closed won deal from it should count against January ad spend.
Is ad click data persisting to opportunity records?	You need to be able to see which ads and ad-sets drove your closed won deals.
Are you collecting the lead information you need to make decisions?	Generally, it is hard to optimize campaigns without collecting rich lead data at the start of your funnel first.

Resources & Extras

Making sense of buzzwords

B2B marketing is a buzzword-heavy field. In this book, we've defined the most relevant ones, those that truly contribute to the art and science of B2B marketing and shown you how to apply them in your business. There are few others that are worth calling out, not because they're helpful or important, but because they cause confusion and frequently show up in hashtags and bad advice from LinkedIn influencers. I keep bringing up myth-busting because a big part of the reason I decided to write this book is to help advertisers distinguish what's real from what's a flash in the pan. That's why the title is *Do What Works* because the principles presented here have been proven to work, with a decade of evidence and earned wisdom to back up the claims I make here. The problem with buzzwords is they present a too-easy alternative where a cute turn of phrase and a life hack has taken the place of methodology and an evidence-based approach.

"**Dark Social**" is a big one with a cult following. It comes from the "you can't track anything on LinkedIn" crowd. The basic idea is that you can't track B2B ad results, and no one actually fills out lead forms, so you should just post organically and hope for the best, while also doing some light targeting of ABM lists. This strategy has its place, but it's hard to scale because it doesn't have an effective feedback loop. The worst thing about the Dark Social evangelists is not the tactics themselves, but their rejection of all of the other tools B2B advertisers have.

Misleading labels—There's a whole suite of terms that aren't wrong, but it's important to know that they draw false distinctions around artificial categories. I'm talking about **demand gen vs. lead gen** and **brand marketing vs direct response.** These can feel like separate buckets or entirely separate strategies, but really, they're all part of B2B marketing with different uses for different times. It's not that one is right and one is wrong. This goes back to some of the charts we looked at earlier covering the right channel for the right audience size.

Where online influencers steer you wrong is when they say "lead gen is totally wrong if you're just generating MQLs and sending them to your sales team. That's old school and it doesn't work." That's not true. We see that work all the time, but you just have to know when to apply each tactic. The same goes for brand vs direct response marketing. They're different tactics that both help you accomplish the same goal: generating revenue for your business. The important lesson for marketers is knowing when and how to use them, not which is better.

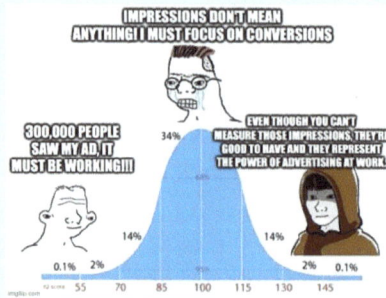

Ideally, advertising can become a greater part of your marketing mix over time because it has a higher marginal value than anything else you can spend money on or put effort in.

The average B2B company probably gets 10% of their new business from advertising, but the optimized B2B business can get 50% of their new business from advertising because it's such a scalable channel. So that gap—between 10-50%—should be where you aim.

That gap is a big one, and the difference matters. If you're running a division responsible for 10% of your company's revenue, that's great. They appreciate you, no doubt. If you're generating 20, 30, or 50% of the company's revenue, all of a sudden, you're very important and making a big difference to the future outcome of that company and, therefore, making a bigger impact on the world because that company is doing something that people are responding to.

So that's the real impact of advertising beyond just ROI. In the long term, there are a lot of benefits you can't see that we haven't covered much in this book because you can't measure them and, therefore, can't be strategic about them. Your ads will educate and add value through your offers, even in the lives of those who don't convert. These are the sprinkles we don't talk about because we're in the business of measuring the ice cream.

In the end, these unquantifiables all come full-circle and matter a lot, even though you may learn to ignore them in the process of creating L.I.F.E. It's like midtwit meme. People who are really unsophisticated about marketing get excited about impressions, like, "oh man, 300,000 people saw this!" Then, as you become an experienced practitioner, you realize impressions don't mean anything, and you learn to just focus on conversions. But the truly wise advertiser knows that even though you can't measure those impressions, they're good to have, and they represent the power of advertising at work.

Brand-building with B2B ads

(*These tips were originally featured as a Right Percent B2B Guide in our B2B Resource Base*)

So far, we've looked at the problems with confusing brand goals and B2B ad goals, but that's not to say there isn't tremendous value in branding done right, or that B2B ads can't be a part of your brand-building strategy.

We've covered how B2B brand campaigns go wrong. Just to recap, the main problem we see is when businesses optimize for top-of-funnel metrics like views or clicks which give a weak algorithmic signal. This means even if you're targeting a good audience, your spend is largely wasted on the least-qualified members of your audience. Platform auctions further exacerbate this problem.

B2B brand Advertising done right

There are two ways to make brand advertising work.

1. **Precise audiences**—If you have small, proven audiences, you don't have to rely on the algorithmic feedback loop nearly as much. A proven audience is one that worked well for you for direct response campaigns or worked well for targeting with your sales team.

2. This is basically the same as an AMB strategy: get a precise list of accounts, hit them with a series of ads, and measure the overall impact at the end.

3. **Top-of-funnel content**—If you're going to promote to a large audience, instead of optimizing for a top-of-funnel event, where there's no feedback loop, optimize for an event where you can still qualify the user. Content, eBooks, tools, and templates all work so long as there is a qualification step you can tag. As a bonus, this will also get you some direct response results too. You can still measure this campaign like a Brand campaign to make sure you're seeing the full funnel impact of your work.

Measuring brand campaign results

Usually, brand advertising performance is measured in one of three ways:

1. **Simple top-of-funnel metrics**—How many views, clicks, and video watches your campaign received. This is not a useful metric because we don't have any way to verify that these views and clicks are really from our target customer.

2. **Survey before and after**—If we survey users before and after the Brand spend, does it show improved survey results after the spend? Surveys are not great for B2B for the same reason—the algorithms are even worse at determining that survey participants are in your ICP than they are at selecting them as ad clickers.

3. **Lift test**—Did we see a lift in company metrics in the time/place we ran the test? This is the golden metric for measuring brand

campaigns. Specifically, geography-based lift tests. You need to make sure you have enough data in your test geographies to get statistically significant conclusions.

Be cautious with influencers

We covered some buzzwords and misconceptions. But when it comes to LinkedIn influencers and their hot takes, it's worth backing up to consider the medium and its potentially harmful effects on users looking for good advice.

It's almost inevitable that influencers will go after the lowest common denominator because they're addicted to getting more likes, and to do that, they have to go broad with their content and, in many cases, be deliberately controversial. While a post on *how to optimize your B2B ads* might get five likes, the bold claim that *nobody wants to see gated content* might set off a firestorm of debate in the comments among a mixed audience of B2B and non-B2B people that will drive more eyeballs to this low-value clickbait. "Beef" marketing, where you get attention by starting fights, works. There are always going to be people vying for attention by taking shots at boring but effective best-practices.

The annoying thing is that it's really hard for a layperson to tell the difference between valuable contrarianism, like some of the arguments presented in this book, and clickbait from LinkedIn influencers who don't know what they're talking about. It's tough out there.

How to be your agency's favorite client

The best agencies/client relationships are approached as partnerships and collaborations. We're here to help you. The best thing you can do for us is to focus on all the internal stuff that's hard for us to manage. For example, we can help advise on offers, but as an internal stakeholder, one of your most important jobs is coordinating with teams and making sure, okay, what offers do we have available? What content can we promote? Generally, the client is responsible for making their own offers, so the more you can do on that end, the better.

Attribution is another big one. You have a ton of data inside your company that we may need to work out how things are being tracked and what might be broken. We can help you navigate all of that, but attribution and tracking are somewhat owned by your brand, not by an agency—and you wouldn't want them to be, because that would mean you don't have control over your own data.

We've talked a lot about the importance of a strong link between marketing and sales, and it's better if that is an internal link rather than someone at a third-party agency.

There's no easy way to say this, but for most clients, our job is getting them out of their own way. One thing you can do to help us help you in that regard is to streamline communication. Remove everyone from the comms loop who doesn't need to be in it, and make a clear, single point of contact in charge of approving creative and campaigns.

We have learned the hard way that it's always better to go deeper with the team you have rather than adding to your team.

Fast and light should be the goal, always.

The morality of B2B advertising

Are people tracking you?

Is your data being sold?

Is there an FBI agent living in your phone who knows everything you do online?

These questions have chilling effects on development teams who have an aversion to certain types of tracking—not because of a regulation against it, but basically because it gives them the heebie-jeebies.

It's too bad because the modern tracking of Facebook, Google, and LinkedIn is really incredible, and they aren't the boogiemen they're sometimes portrayed as.

The biggest myth here is that Facebook sells your data. They don't. Facebook keeps your data internally, which is the most valuable asset it has. What they do is rent the ability to advertise to you on their platform on an aggregate level. That's very different from saying, "here you go, target Joe Schmoe who likes this type of chocolate and drives this kind of car."

Many people who find algorithms unsettling may not realize that long before the internet, direct mail marketers could buy lists from InfoGroup with the estimated credit scores, home addresses, and job titles of 5 million Americans—all for just pennies on the dollar. These lists still exist. People are out there selling your data, but nobody cares. It's just like how the phone books used to publish your phone number without your permission, and you had to ask to be taken off the list. Google, Facebook, and LinkedIn aren't doing anything like that. Not only that, but these big three ad platforms do an amazing job of keeping your data safe. Google and Facebook haven't had a data breach in years. And anyone interested in using your data for surveillance, or other sinister purposes can easily find it elsewhere. Your internet service provider has a full and detailed record of every internet search you've ever done and every webpage you've ever visited. Whereas the data Facebook provides advertisers is aggregated and anonymized. So, the idea that advertising is somehow compromising your privacy in some way is just frankly silly. There is no harm done from personalized advertising on Facebook, Google, and LinkedIn that I have found beyond the impact of whatever it is you're selling.

And by the way, you're voluntarily using these platforms for fun and information and socializing and browsing. The only reason these products are free is because advertising supports them, and that's part of the deal you make.

The future of B2B advertising

The future is algorithmic.

Ten years ago, Facebook pioneered algorithmic advertising where you don't need precise targeting, you don't need lists. You can have a big audience and the platform will find your conversions for you. Google soon followed that path and became really good at it. LinkedIn is far behind, but they have a bunch of products going in that direction. The future is more algorithmic. Knowing how to manipulate those black boxes, how to use conversion events, and how to use those platforms to get signals is all very important now and will be even more important in the near future. Regulation around tracking and the crackdown on the pixel in Europe, California, and beyond will only accelerate this trend and widen the gap between those who can make the algorithm work for them and those who can't.

We're also seeing a trend where people don't want to leave the platform they're on, and, of course, the platforms don't want them to leave either. To keep you engaged, Facebook and LinkedIn are degrading eternal links as they realize users would rather keep scrolling and stay in their feeds. This will lead to further consolidation of content across channels and make blogs less appealing as content assets for businesses and reading material for social media users.

AI will clearly continue to have a big impact, contributing to more advanced targeting and automation. As Mark Zuckerberg pointed out recently, in the future, you'll just pick your budget, pick your goal, and Facebook will take care of everything, including creative.

Some marketers are afraid of this future, especially ones for whom media buying was a big part of their skillset. A lot of performance marketers were almost offended by Performance Max, which is a relatively new ad unit at Google which is all algorithmic and doesn't give you much control. It's a little scary if you've spent a decade or more of your career learning exactly which buttons to click and what manual choices to make. It feels like you're being replaced by an algorithm. Personally, I've never found that the media buying choices were the most important part. It's more about understanding the whole of it. The tools will always be changing, but the purpose you use them for will remain the same: bringing customers in.

Even with AI doing a lot of it for you, there's plenty of work to do.

Cut through the noise with Right Percent

The goal of this book was to include everything you need to know in order to develop and run effective B2B ads campaigns. But if what you've read makes you think, *I need to hire professionals to run my campaign*, we hope you give Right Percent a call.

Right Percent stands out for three key reasons

Laser focus on B2B advertising

We have spent nearly six years specializing in B2B performance ads across LinkedIn, Meta, Google, and more, managing over $150 million in ad spend. Right Percent focuses solely on delivering faster growth and better ROI through the power of B2B advertising.

A senior-only team

Every team member has at least seven years of ad experience—no juniors, no middlemen, and no wasted time. This means expert execution and direct access to specialists who know exactly what they're doing.

Flexible access to top talent

As part of Right Side Up, we can bring in the best specialists (e.g., podcast experts, Amazon strategists, longform lead-gen content creators) under one contract. Clients get full transparency—knowing exactly who will manage their account and even interviewing them beforehand.

Additionally, our deep B2B expertise extends beyond just in-platform ads management but also the specialized copywriting, creative strategy, and attribution that make ads programs work. While digital ads might seem straightforward, success requires expert handling to adapt to market changes, avoid costly mistakes, and make the right strategic decisions. Right Percent ensures your ad budget delivers maximum impact.

To get started with Right Percent, go to RigthtPercent.com/contact-us.

Appendix A

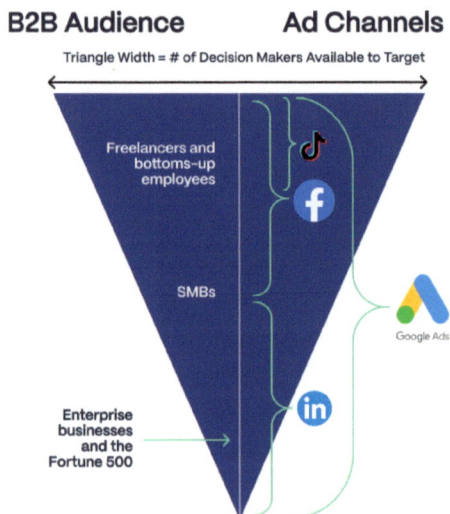

B2B audience size impacts
channel ad strategy

B2B Audience   **Ad Channels**

Triangle Width = # of Decision Makers Available to Target

Freelancers and bottoms-up employees

SMBs

Enterprise businesses and the Fortune 500

B2B audience size impacts
targeting strategy

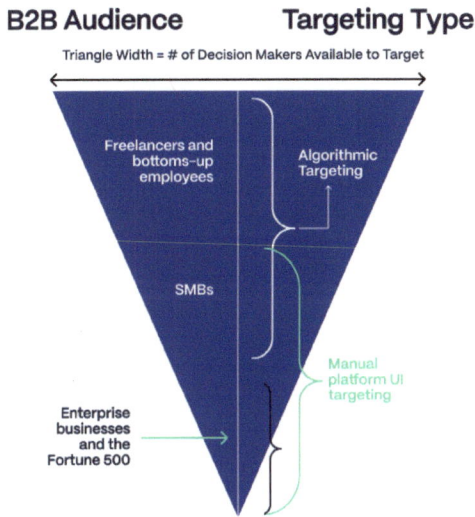

B2B Audience **Targeting Type**

Triangle Width = # of Decision Makers Available to Target

Freelancers and bottoms-up employees

Algorithmic Targeting

SMBs

Manual platform UI targeting

Enterprise businesses and the Fortune 500

What four **levers** do B2B marketing leaders have to beat **paid media goals**?

Test different **audiences** and/or keywords.

Test different **offers** and experiences in your ads.

Systematize making **ad creative and copy.**

Test new **conversion events** to optimize on.

The Formula for a Successful B2B Ad Campaign

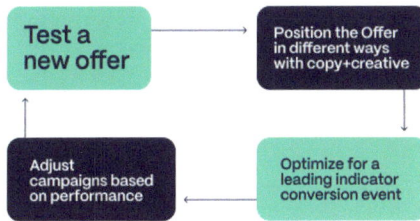

```
┌─────────────┐        ┌──────────────────────┐
│  Test a     │──────▶ │ Position the Offer    │
│  new offer  │        │ in different ways     │
└─────────────┘        │ with copy+creative    │
       ▲               └──────────────────────┘
       │                          │
       │                          ▼
┌──────────────────┐   ┌──────────────────────┐
│ Adjust           │   │ Optimize for a        │
│ campaigns based  │◀──│ leading indicator     │
│ on performance   │   │ conversion event      │
└──────────────────┘   └──────────────────────┘
```

What do you need to know?

1. Offers can be a product, landing page, piece of content or incentive – whatever you're promoting.

2. By testing Offer positioning, you see whats most appealing to your audience.

3. Your conversion event has to be a leading indicator of future revenue or your campaign will be hard to prove out.

B2B ad accounts should be anti-cyclical in Q4 - reduce budgets from mid-Nov to mid-Dec, then accelerate

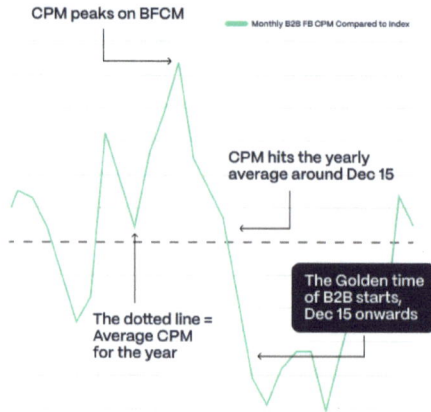

CPM peaks on BFCM

Monthly B2B FB CPM Compared to Index

CPM hits the yearly average around Dec 15

The dotted line = Average CPM for the year

The Golden time of B2B starts, Dec 15 onwards

The **right conversion event** can dramatically improve **B2B lead quality.**

→ Both of the below B2B advertising campaigns used the **same targeting** and the **same creative assets.**

→ But Campaign B generated **many more qualified leads** because it only fired lead conversion events to Facebook **if they met certain criteria.**

	Spend	Leads	CPL	Highly Qualified Leads	CPHQL
Campaign A Optimizing towards leads	$99,565	13,829	$7	343	$291
Campaign B Optimizing towards highly qualified leads	$101,565	9,173	$11	1,565	$65

What four **levers** do you have to improve lead quality?

Make **creative** that makes qualified users self-select.

Optimize towards a **conversion event** that correlates to revenue.

Promote **content** that appeals to qualified users.

Target narrower **audiences** and/or keywords.

B2B audience size impacts
ad strategy

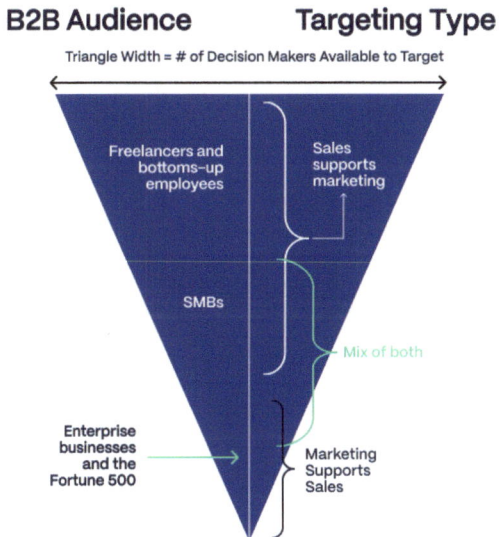

B2B Audience   Targeting Type

Triangle Width = # of Decision Makers Available to Target

Freelancers and bottoms–up employees

Sales supports marketing

SMBs

Mix of both

Enterprise businesses and the Fortune 500

Marketing Supports Sales

B2B audience size impacts
content strategy

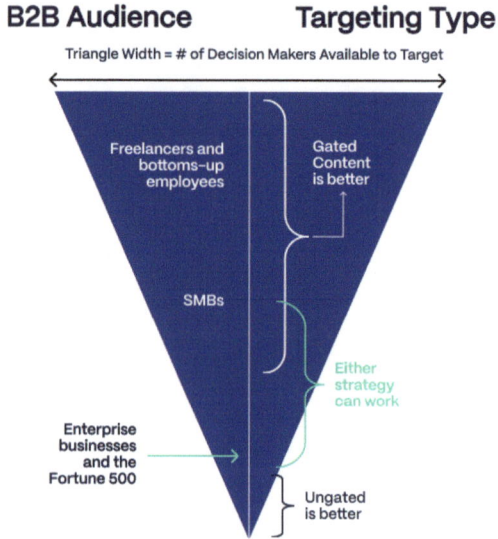

B2B Audience　　　**Targeting Type**

Triangle Width = # of Decision Makers Available to Target

Freelancers and
bottoms–up
employees

Gated
Content
is better

SMBs

Either
strategy
can work

Enterprise
businesses
and the
Fortune 500

Ungated
is better

Should your org be more sales led or marketing led?

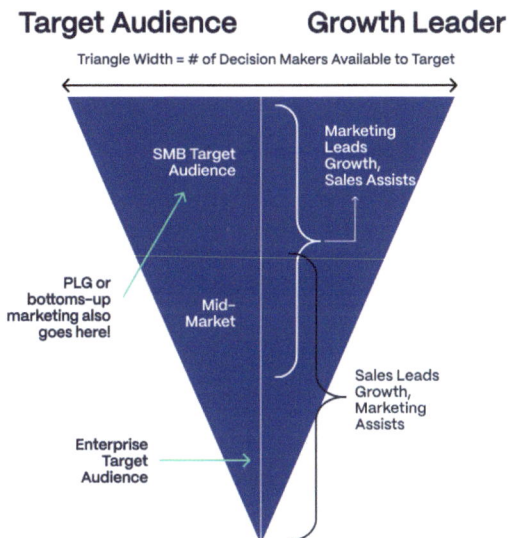

Target Audience   **Growth Leader**

Triangle Width = # of Decision Makers Available to Target

SMB Target Audience

Marketing Leads Growth, Sales Assists

PLG or bottoms-up marketing also goes here!

Mid–Market

Sales Leads Growth, Marketing Assists

Enterprise Target Audience

What's the ideal structure of a B2B demand gen team?

Marketing Lead

Key Skill: Understanding distribution and nurture channel dynamics

Distribution Channel Experts	Nurture Channel Experts	Marketing Support
Paid Search & Social	Email Marketing	MarOps
SEO & Organic	Content Creation	Marketing Engineering
Many other possibilities	Many other possibilities	Creative & Copy

The Virtuous Cycle of B2B Online Advertising

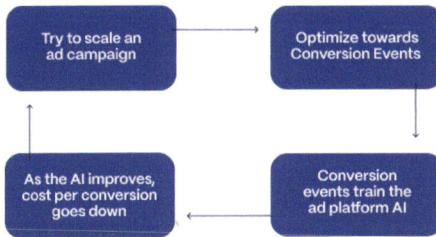

What do you need to make the virtuous cycle work?

(1) A conversion event that correlates to downfunnel revenue – training the AI to generate leads that don't convert doesn't help.

(2) Creative that attracts qualified leads and sign-ups.

(3) At least 30 conversion events per week, preferably 50.

Formal ad test tracking spreadsheets don't work well

- In the long run, 10% of the ads and tests you run on Facebook, LinkedIn and Google will generate 90% of your revenue. Most will generate close to no spend or results.

- This means most tests will not get significant data, and the winners will be very obvious.

- This is why "test measurement" spreadsheets – where people track hypotheses, tests, future results, etc. – end up being not very useful.

- In my experience a better way of keeping track of wins in a shareable format is a quarterly report that takes account of failed tests and focuses on the big wins.

B2B audience size impacts **average cost per lead.**

It costs more to get enterprise leads than SMB, and more to get SMB than freelance or bottoms–up leads. There's just more dollars competing for fewer decision makers.

The fewer decision makers in your target audience, the higher the cost per lead

Average Cost Per Lead   Number of Decision Makers

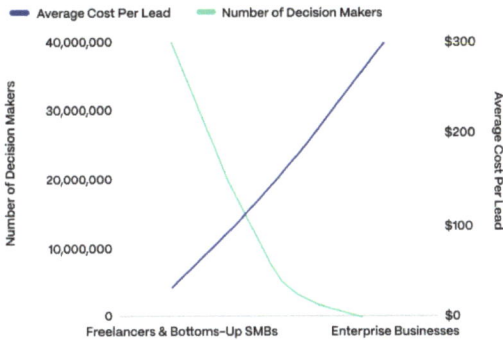

What's the structure of your RP team?

Strategist

A strategist deeply understands **B2B advertising** and the **RP method.**

Distribution Channel Experts

B2B Search Specialist

Facebook Ads Specialist

LinkedIn Ads Specialist

B2B Support Team

Creative Director

Copywriter

Attribution & Data

What makes **B2B paid search** different than **consumer focused paid search?**

Two key ingredients to successful digital B2B advertising:

| Potential customer intent | Potential customer level of qualification |

Someone using Adwords to sell consumer goods, like kitchen toasters, only has to worry about intent. There may be some preference variation but by-and-large if the intent is there you can convert a good amount of those searchers.

B2B Adwords advertisers have to add qualification to the mix If you're selling commercial coffee grinders to coffee shops, you don't want to pay Google for clicks from people buying personal coffee grinders for their home kitchens.

How to make winning SEM ads for B2B

The most significant difference for B2B ads is **qualification**. If non-target searchers can use the search terms you're using, make sure to make your ad title explicitly quality users.

Imagine you're selling a software for preschools or other child care centers. You're targeting the keyword, "Preschool Software".

Bad headline:

"Preschool Made Easy" — Any parents that happen to be searching for personal software, like at-home preschool learning videos, will click this.

Okay headline:

"Preschool Software" — Better, but you still are going to get some bad clicks.

Good Headline:

"Preschool Management Software" — Management is a boring word — perfect!

Gated content **prevents ad fatigue** in B2B ad accounts.

Below is aggregated data. Ad accounts that only use "get a demo" ads and no content ads face headwinds from audience fatigue.

Click Through Rate of Ad Accounts over Time

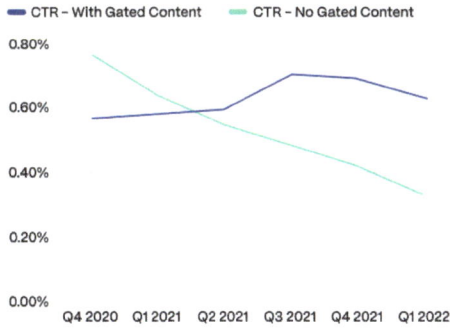

▬ CTR – With Gated Content   ▬ CTR – No Gated Content

0.80%	
0.60%	
0.40%	
0.20%	
0.00%	Q4 2020 Q1 2021 Q2 2021 Q3 2021 Q4 2021 Q1 2022

Appendix B

Reddit reaches real buyers while they're making decisions.

79% of users want to hear from brands.

r/PetAdvice

r/Pets

r/catcare

Get **$500 in ad credit** when you spend $500 →

Reddit reaches real buyers while they're making decisions.

79% of users want to hear from brands.

9:41

u/campglow Promoted

For camping or glamping, Camp Glow lanterns are lit. Sustainable, impact-resistant, and stormproof.

campglow.com   Shop No

Get **$500 in ad credit** when you spend $500 →

Reach over 100k active communities with Reddit ads.

Get your brand in front of audiences you won't find elsewhere.

Get **$500 in ad credit** when you spend $500.

Get started

r/Streetwear

Reddit ranks #1 in trust for product research.

Even ahead of Google.

Reddit ranks #1 in trust for product research.

Even ahead of Google.

Marketing Managers:
Find your best ROAS with full-funnel targeting.

Get $500 in ad credit when you spend $500.

r/patientgamers
r/battlestations
r/ShouldIbuythis
r/gaymers
r/letsplay
r/retrogaming
r/gaming
r/truegaming

Whether you're selling software or skincare, Reddit just works.

r/Skincare_Addiction
r/pcgaming
r/outfitoftheday

SPF: Your summer BFF.

Spend $500 and get $500 in ad credit →

Whether you're selling software or skincare, Reddit just works.

SUPER STAY
MAYBELLINE NEW YORK

Spend $500 and get $500 in ad credit →

Keyword
Interests
Behavior
Demographics

Marketers

Get $500 in ad credit when you spend $500!

Get Started →

Simple setup. High-trust environment.

Stronger purchase intent.

Reddit is everything an SMB needs to grow.

r/fashionadvice
r/Streetwear
r/SneakerDeals

Simple setup. High-trust environment.
Stronger purchase intent.

Reddit is everything an SMB needs to grow.

business

Target your most valuable customers where buying decisions happen

Advertise on Reddit. Get $500 in ad credit when you spend $500

Get started

Built for Small Teams. Backed by Real Results.

- Launch ads in minutes — no agency required
- Reach high-intent users in topic-based communities
- Get $500 in ad credit when you spend $500

Carousel

Built for Small Teams. Backed by Real Results.

- Launch ads in minutes — no agency required
- Reach high-intent users in topic-based communities
- Get $500 in ad credit when you spend $500

Marketers:
Get $500 in ad credit when you spend $500

34% of Redditors aren't on Facebook.
52% aren't on TikTok.
72% aren't on LinkedIn.

r/pcmasterrace

reddit for business

HR DIRECTORS:

LEVEL UP YOUR WORKFORCE, LOWER YOUR RISK.

Velocity Global

"Our CEO loves the fact that working with Velocity Global means we don't need to handle everything ourselves, employ HR people in-country, or worry about compliance. The price you pay is well worth removing all that headache and stress.

Ellen Bockelman
Chief People Officer

Velocity Global

Velocity Global

GROW YOUR GLOBAL WORKFORCE. LIGHTEN YOUR WORKLOAD.

Free Guide: Hire Everywhere, Go Anywhere.

THE (HIRING) WORLD IS YOURS.
Download our free guide & grow your workforce.

Velocity Global

Velocity Global

FREE GUIDE

HIRE EVERYWHERE, GO ANYWHERE.

Download Guide

Fleet Managers:
Get your free evaluation guide now. Learn how to assess:

- ☑ Fleet compatibility
- ☑ Hardware considerations
- ☑ Potential ROI
- ☑ Long-term scalability

ʍotive

Velocity Global

ONLY 35% OF EXECUTIVES FEEL CONFIDENT THEY CAN QUICKLY SCALE THEIR TALENT NEEDS.

Download Guide

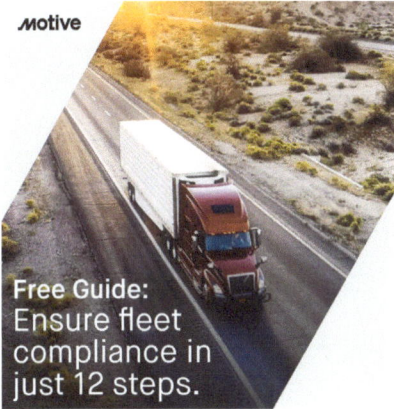

Free Guide:
Ensure fleet compliance in just 12 steps.

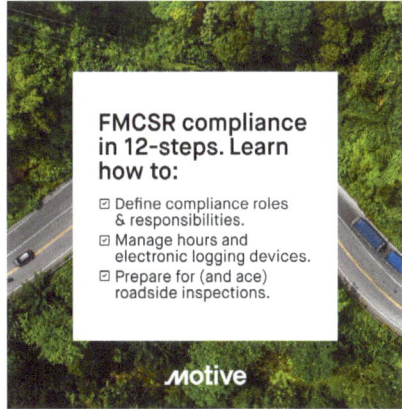

FMCSR compliance in 12-steps. Learn how to:

☑ Define compliance roles & responsibilities.
☑ Manage hours and electronic logging devices.
☑ Prepare for (and ace) roadside inspections.

Experts agree.
Our AI Dashcam ranks #1

Free Guide:
Increase your fuel ROI. Save up to 30,000 gallons per fleet per year.

Is your fleet FMCSR complaint? You can't afford to miss this guide.

Compliance 101.
How to run a compliant fleet in 12 easy steps.

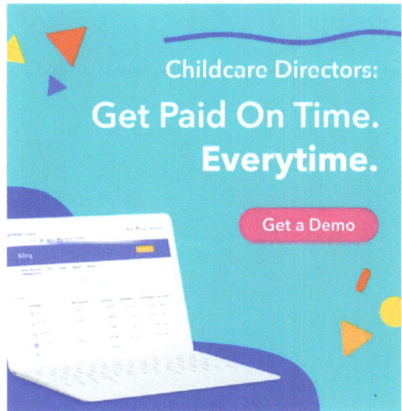

Childcare Directors:
Get Paid On Time. Everytime.

Get a Demo

Childcare Directors:

Use this free checklist to set your staff up for success at your center!

Childcare Directors

Stop wasting time in spreadsheets and get back to doing what you love.

Get your free Financial Peace of Mind templates now!

- Budget planner
- Strategies for late pickup fees & policies
- Tax Preparation Checklist
- Template for changing tuition rates
- Childcare staff salary guide

---

brightwheel

Childcare Directors:

A great onboarding experience creates a healthy, engaged, and productive staff culture.

Get your free staff onboarding checklist now.

You focus on your students, we'll focus on the rest.

brightwheel

"ProsperOps has gone out of their way to understand our business and work to find the best solutions for us. I would enthusiastically recommend their service to anyone looking at a large AWS investment."

David Stanley
Engineering Leader at Webflow

ProsperOps

Supercharge your CMP

Get Started

ProsperOps

Experience Cloud Savings as a Service with a free savings analysis

- Benchmark your performance vs. peers
- Get setup and running in minutes
- See your quantitative savings potential

ProsperOps

Managing AWS costs internally? You're leaving money on the table.

Join the top 2% of cloud FinOps teams.

ProsperOps

Experience Cloud Savings as a Service with a free savings analysis

- Benchmark your performance vs. peers
- Get setup and running in minutes
- See your quantitative savings potential

ProsperOps

Managing AWS costs internally? You're leaving money on the table.

Join the top 2% of cloud FinOps teams.

ProsperOps

Managing AWS costs internally?

You're leaving money on the table.
Outperform 98% of cloud FinOps teams.

ProsperOps

Maximize your cloud savings. Get your free savings analysis now.

No write permissions required.

ProsperOps

Marketing Leaders: air.inc

Never lose another visual asset in Dropbox.

air.inc

Find and share visual assets in seconds.

Creative reviews, feedback and approvals in minutes, not days.

Food&Art Magazine
3MB · 480 × 480
Ready for print

Partnerships
3MB · 480 × 480
In review

Photoshooting
3MB · 480 × 480
Ready to post

Visual asset file management without the confusion.

air.inc

Macarons
3MB · 480 × 480
Approved · Brooklyn

Blueberry cupcake
3MB · 480 × 480
In review · Brooklyn

air.inc

Tired of sorting through 638 visual assets to find the one you need?

You need Air.

Monstera
3MB · 480 × 480
Ready to post · NYC

Mixed plants
3MB · 480 × 480
Ready for print

Mixed plants
3MB · 480 × 480
Ready for print · NYC

8000+ videos and images.

1 visual asset management platform.

0 stress.

Social assets
3MB · 480 × 480
Ready to post

Social assets
3MB · 480 × 480
Ready to post

Mismanaging your cashflow can bankrupt your business.

Business Owners:
Mismanaging your cashflow can bankrupt your business.

betterfin
Get 3 essential cashflow reports for your business

Business Owners:

Get 3 essential cashflow reports for your business

betterfin

BOULEVARD

The Ultimate Growth Playbook for Beauty Businesses

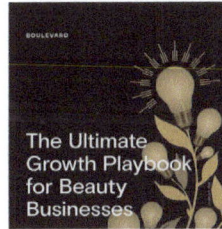

BOULEVARD

The Ultimate Growth Playbook for Beauty Businesses

When to open a new beauty business location

BOULEVARD

How to Run a Spa
(without running yourself ragged)

BOULEVARD

BOULEVARD

Beauty business owners that use Boulevard have:

16%
more services booked

71%
fewer no-shows and late cancels

18%
more retail value

24%
more gratuity from clients

Beauty Professionals:

✦ **Eliminate Appointment Gaps**

BOULEVARD

SALON & SPA OWNERS:

Reduce No-Shows & Late Cancellations by 71% ✦

BOULEVARD

SALON & SPA OWNERS:

The online booking platform that actually works!

BOULEVARD

SENIOR PRODUCT MANAGERS:

Companies like Shortcut, HashiCorp, & Netlify make their products better with CommandBar.

Shortcut   HashiCorp   netlify

Useful & Beautiful

That's how UX in 2022 is done.

CommandBar

An easy-to-deploy
**command &
search widget**

CommandBar

SENIOR PRODUCT MANAGERS:

Reduce product friction with CommandBar

CommandBar

CommandBar helps users find your product's best features

CommandBar

empeon

HCM HR & Payroll Software
Tailored to Your Healthcare Team
Affordable + White Glove Service

GET $100
AFTER A DEMO

$100

empeon

HR payroll software
Tailored to your healthcare team
Affordable + white glove service

GET $100 AFTER A DEMO

HR payroll software
Tailored to your healthcare team
Affordable + white glove service

GET $100 AFTER A DEMO

empeon

- ⊘ HR payroll software
- ⊘ Tailored to your healthcare team
- ⊘ Affordable + white glove service

empeon

GET $100
AFTER A DEMO

empeon

- ⊘ HR payroll software
- ⊘ Tailored to your healthcare team
- ⊘ Affordable + white glove service

Get $100 after a demo

The financial platform built for e-commerce

JUNI

The financial platform built for e-commerce

JUNI

The financial platform built for e-commerce

JUNI

The financial platform built for e-commerce

JUNI

The financial platform built for e-commerce

The financial platform built for e-commerce

JUNI

The financial platform built for e-commerce

JUNI

Owner

This restaurant made over $450,000 in sales through their website.

See how they did it.

Owner

This restaurant made over $450,000 in sales through their website.

Curious?

Learn more

This restaurant made over $450,000 in sales through their website – and you can too.

Owner

This restaurant made over $450,000 in sales through their website.

See how they did it.

Owner

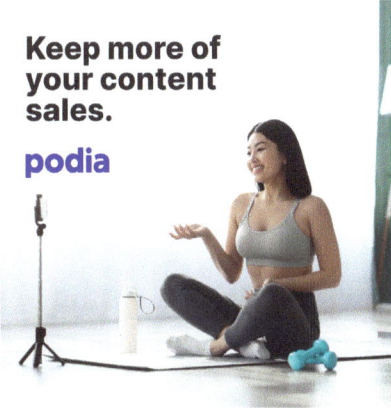

Keep more of your content sales.

podia

Sell all your work on one platform.

podia

Wasteful spending? Not with **this** corporate card.

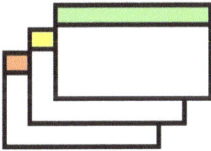

Get $100 and get corporate spending under control with Ramp.

ramp 𝄢   Learn more →

Get $100 and get corporate spending under control with Ramp.

We'll give you a $250 gift card just for signing up for Ramp.

Learn more →

Reducing corporate spending AND get **1.5% cash back** on every purchase.

Learn more →

Switch to a **better** corporate card.

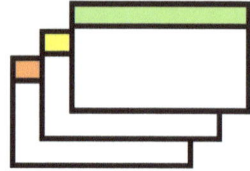

Save your accountants **60 days** per year.

ramp

Control corporate spending and get **1.5% cash back.**

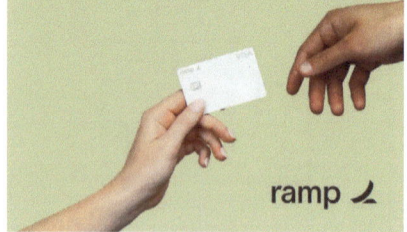

ramp

Cutting corporate spending, now **easier** than ever.

Learn more →

ramp

recharge

#1 for 1,100+ reasons

★★★★★

" Recharge has been awesome for our business, significantly improving our subscription offering for customers and our team. Their customer service is always helpful and solution seeking. "

HUBBLE

17k+ subscribers acquired in the first 3 months

600+ orders processed per day

$1M ↑ run rate each month

with *recharge*

AUTOBRUSH

AutoBrush increased their subscription revenue by

+1300%

with *recharge*

Your subscription program with *Recharge*

who gives a crap — **250%** subscription growth

14x CLTV subscriptions vs. one-time — THE ORIGINAL OATLY!

AUTOBRUSH — **1300%** more subscription revenue

recharge

The #1 choice for subscription management

★ ★ ★ ★ ★ (4.7)

#1 *shopifyplus* CERTIFIED APP

15,000 brands and 50 million subscribers rely on us.

Run a subscription business? **Keep subscribers hooked.**

recharge

Retool
"Sorry, we have to push this to the next sprint"
Build business apps 10x faster
Start for Free

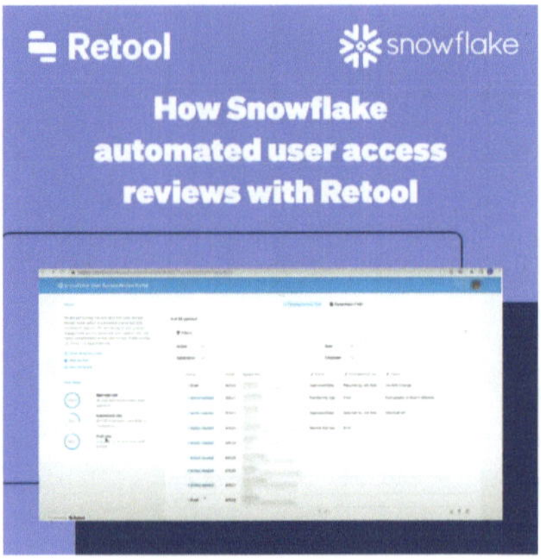
Retool
snowflake
How Snowflake automated user access reviews with Retool

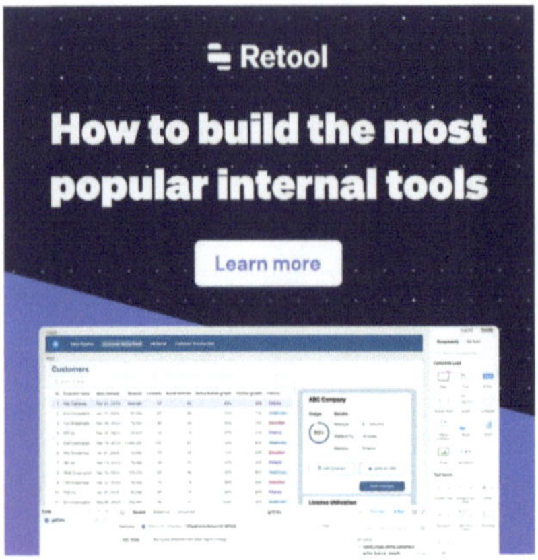
Retool
How to build the most popular internal tools
Learn more

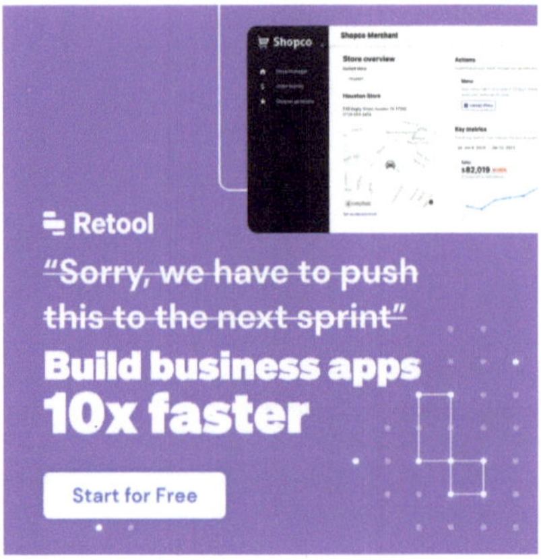
Shopco
Retool
"Sorry, we have to push this to the next sprint"
Build business apps 10x faster
Start for Free

Retool
Technical debt? Never heard of it.
Retool can help you ship new apps or enhance pre-existing apps in hours, not weeks.
Discover Retool

Retool
"Sorry, we have to push this to the next sprint"
Build business apps 10x faster
Start for Free

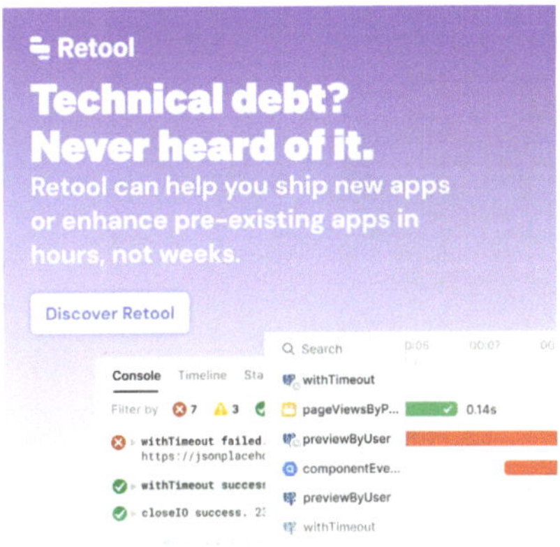

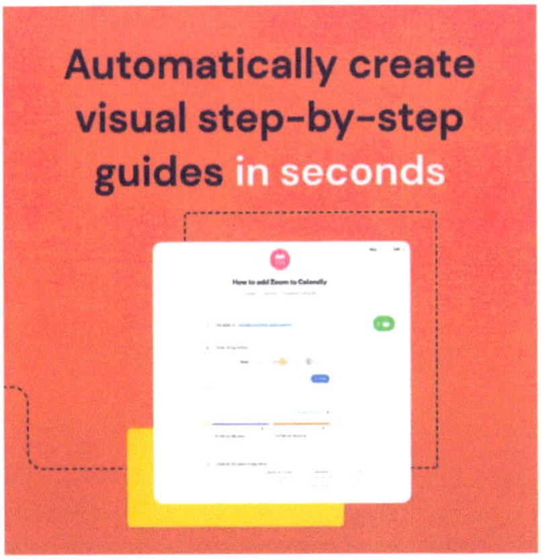

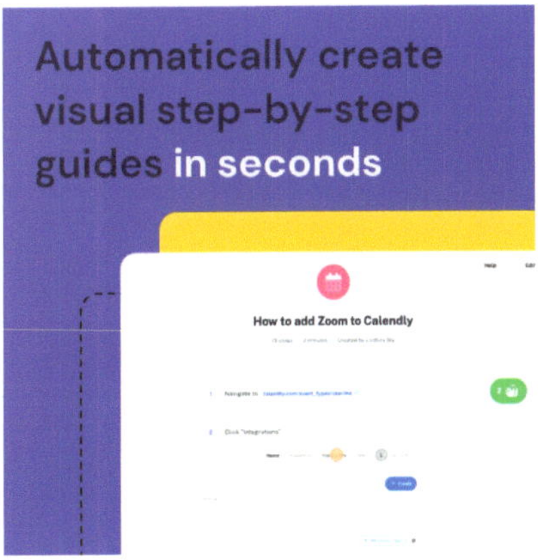

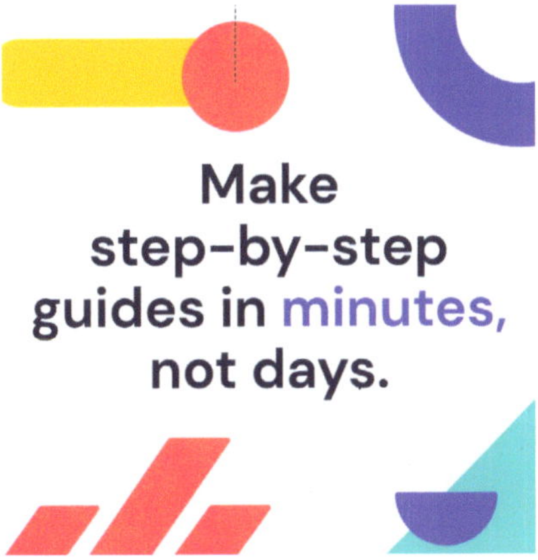

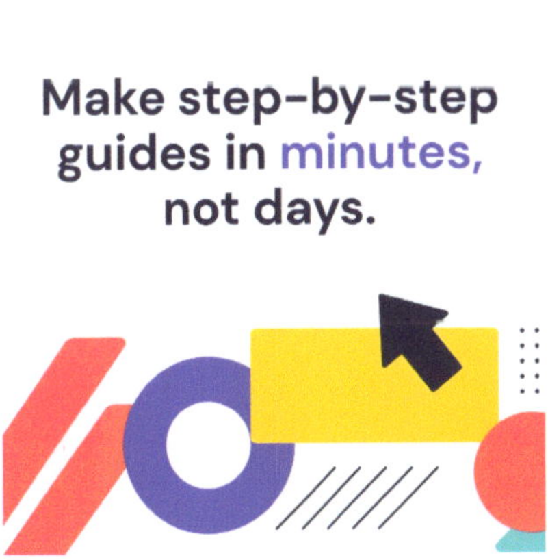

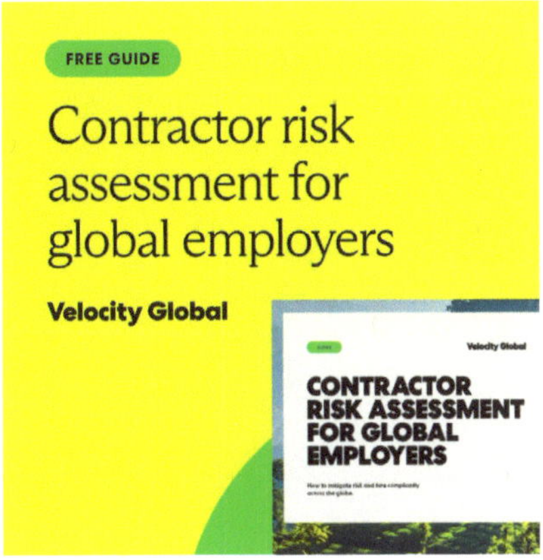

FREE GUIDE

Contractor risk assessment
for global employers

Learn how to:

- Determine if your contractors
  are compliant
- Assess your risk profile
- Fix contractor misclassification

Velocity Global

www.ingramcontent.com/pod-product-compliance
Lightning Source LLC
Chambersburg PA
CBHW041004210326
41597CB00001B/8